GEOGRAPHY Direct

Gary Cambers
Guthlaxton College,
Leicester

Stuart Currie
Margaret Glen-Bott School,
Nottingham

Series consultant:
Peter McLeod,
Hinde House School, Sheffield

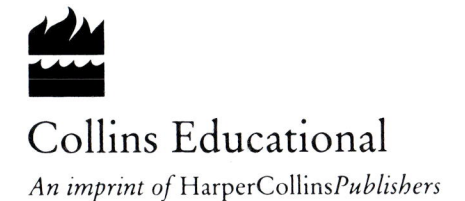

Collins Educational
An imprint of HarperCollins*Publishers*

Contents

Your direct route through Geography 4

Settlement 5
1. Where people live 6
2. Why live there? 8
3. It grew and grew! 10
4. Service with a smile 12
5. Shopping in France 14
6. Shopping around...the city 16
7. Shopping changes 18
8. The changing village 20
9. Getting around 22
10. Using the land 24
11. Land use in a city 26
12. Living in the city 28
13. Changing patterns 30
14. The growing city 32
    Settlement glossary 34
    The next step is yours... 36

Population 37
1. Where is everybody? 38
2. More people are living longer 40
3. People in the countryside 42
4. Living in the city 44
5. People in Europe 46
6. The Ruhr of Germany 48
7. People in French villages 50
8. Change in the UK 52
9. Differences in the UK 54
10. Moving to another country 56
11. A rich society 58
12. The global village 60
    Population glossary 62
    The next step is yours... 64

Earthquakes & Volcanoes 65

1	Natural hazards	66
2	Living dangerously	68
3	Like biting an apple	70
4	Crust factories	72
5	Crust bins	74
6	Waiting for the big one!	76
7	While a country slept...	78
8	Earthquakes: Why Japan?	80
9	Where will the next volcano erupt?	82
10	No skiing today: Eruption in progress	84
11	Volcanoes: Why North Island?	86
12	Volcanoes in Britain!	88
13	Just when you thought it was safe...	90
	Earthquakes & Volcanoes glossary	92
	The next step is yours...	94

What's next? 95

The words explained in the glossaries are underlined the first time that they appear in the text.

All world maps are drawn in Eckert IV projection.

Your direct route through Geography

In studying Geography so far...

- **You have used new words.**

Meander

Pollution

Rain gauge

- **You have looked at different localities.**

What is it?

Why is it changing?

Where is it?

How is it changing?

How did it get like this?

- **You have asked questions.**

Forests burn in Indonesia

New dam threatens tribe in Namibia

Danger to UK countryside

This year you will develop all your skills further when you look at these themes:

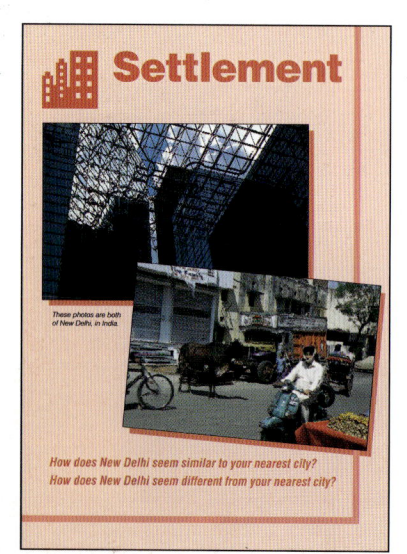

Settlement

These photos are both of New Delhi, in India.

How does New Delhi seem similar to your nearest city?
How does New Delhi seem different from your nearest city?

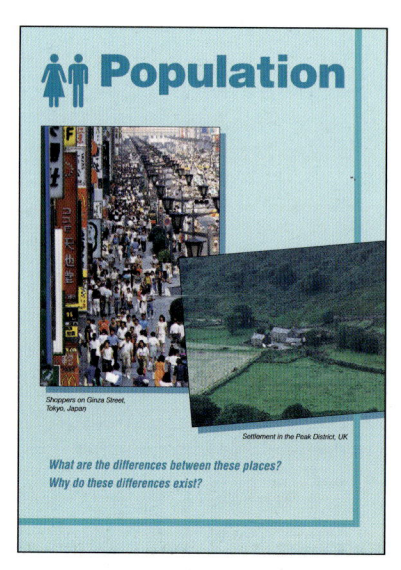

Population

Shoppers on Ginza Street, Tokyo, Japan

Settlement in the Peak District, UK

What are the differences between these places?
Why do these differences exist?

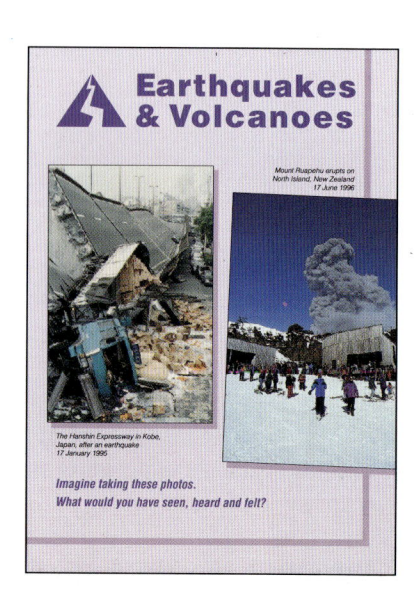

Earthquakes & Volcanoes

Mount Ruapehu erupts on North Island, New Zealand 17 June 1996

The Hanshin Expressway in Kobe, Japan, after an earthquake 17 January 1995

Imagine taking these photos.
What would you have seen, heard and felt?

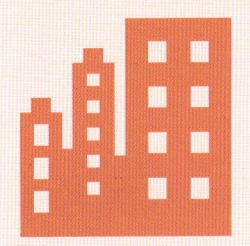

Settlement

These photos are both of New Delhi, in India.

How does New Delhi seem similar to your nearest city?
How does New Delhi seem different from your nearest city?

1 | Where people live

What are settlements?
What is a temporary settlement?
What is a permanent settlement?

The Khampa people of south-west China and Tibet are <u>nomads</u>. They move across the grasslands with their animals. They keep small herds of yaks and goats. When they move, they take their homes with them.

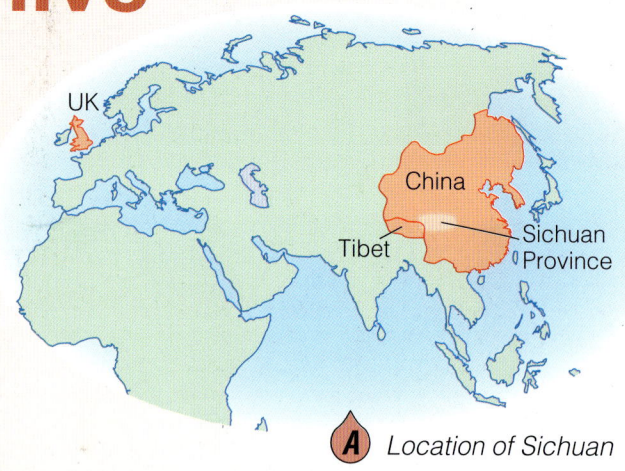

A Location of Sichuan

B A Khampa nomad camp, Sichuan, China

C Cooking inside a Khampa nomad home, Sichuan, China

1 Describe the location of Sichuan Province. Use MAP **A** and an atlas to help you.

2 Study PHOTOS **B** and **C**.
   a Describe the Khampa settlement. Use these headings:
      • size • building materials • space.
   b What is the importance of animals to the Khampa people?

3 a Draw a sketch of PHOTO **C**. Add these labels to your sketch:
      • cooker • pots • pans • chimney.
   b Work out a menu for a three-course meal. Use only food which you think the Khampa people will have.

4 a Explain why nomads like the Khampa need to move.
   b How do you think they may move homes?
   c Does PHOTO **C** show a permanent or temporary settlement?

SETTLEMENT 1

D Kangding settlement, Sichuan, China

E A kitchen in a Chinese flat

Permanent settlements

You live in a settlement. Houses like yours are usually grouped together in permanent settlements. The group of houses in PHOTO *D* is the town of Kangding. It is in Sichuan Province, China. Most of the people of Kangding live in flats.

5 a Study PHOTO *D*. Write a paragraph about this settlement using the headings:
- size
- building materials
- space.

b Discuss the main differences between this settlement and that of the Khampa nomads.

c Is this a permanent or temporary settlement?

6 a Study PHOTO *E*. Compare PHOTOS *E* and *C* by completing the following: The kitchen in the flat has an electric cooker but in the nomad tent people use a wood-burning stove. Other differences include...

b What differences do you think there are in the lives of people in the two settlements?

c How are these settlements
- similar and
- different to the one in which you live?

7 What is a settlement?

7

2 | Why live there?

Where do settlers come from?
What places were important to early settlers?
How are the sites of settlements similar and different?

A Location of Nottingham

People have come to Britain from other places for many years. Some early settlers lived in caves. The first big invasion was by the Romans in AD 43. Several centuries later, the Anglo-Saxons came across the North Sea. One of the many places they settled was Nottingham.

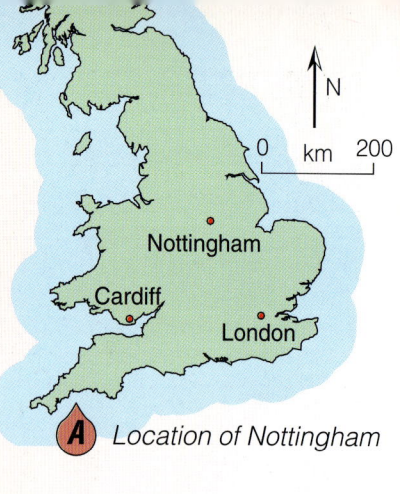

C View from the River Trent to where the Anglo Saxons lived

D Nottingham Castle on top of its steep river cliff

B Aerial view of Nottingham

Most land away from the rivers was forested in Anglo-Saxon times

The flat valley floor south of the castle and Anglo-Saxon town was easily flooded.

A ford is a part of a river which is shallow enough to walk across

---

1 Look at PHOTO **B**. On which river does Nottingham stand?

2 Use PHOTOS **C** and **D**. Discuss why being next to a river was important to early settlers.

3 a How did people first cross the River Trent in this area?
   b Describe how this has now changed.
   c Suggest how West Bridgford got its name.

4 On a copy of PHOTO **B**:
   a label the River Trent, Nottingham Castle, West Bridgford, areas of land which could be easily flooded;
   b add notes which explain why being next to a river was important;
   c finish your work by adding any other notes which explain why people settled at Nottingham.

E *Ely – built on higher ground above all the surrounding marshes* болото

A <u>bridging point</u> is a stretch of river where a bridge could be built across. Some rivers have only a few bridging points. This makes these points very important. In the past, people who controlled a bridging point could become very powerful. сильный

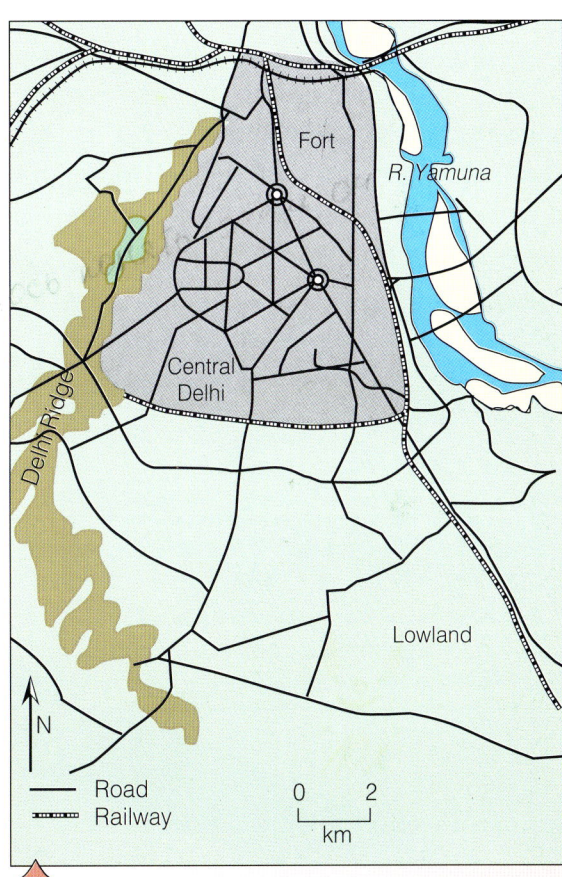

F *Liverpool docks, 1930*

G *Corfe Castle, Dorset*

H *Site of Delhi*

5 Use PHOTOS **E–G** and MAP **H**. With an atlas complete a copy of this table:

Place name	Where is it?	Reason for settlement
Liverpool	On the R. Mersey in NW England	

6 How similar are the reasons for the settlement of Nottingham and Delhi?

7 Choose a settlement near your home. Find out who settled there first and why they settled.

3 It grew and grew!

**Why do some settlements grow?
What is the function of settlements?
How do settlement functions change with time?**

Not all settlements grow. Sometimes the reason for people settling in a place stops being important. The need to control the gap in the hills at Corfe Castle disappeared a long time ago. A new <u>function</u> never took its place, so the small town did not get any bigger. Some places, though, grew much bigger as their functions changed. Many, like Nottingham, developed new industries. More people then moved in to find work.

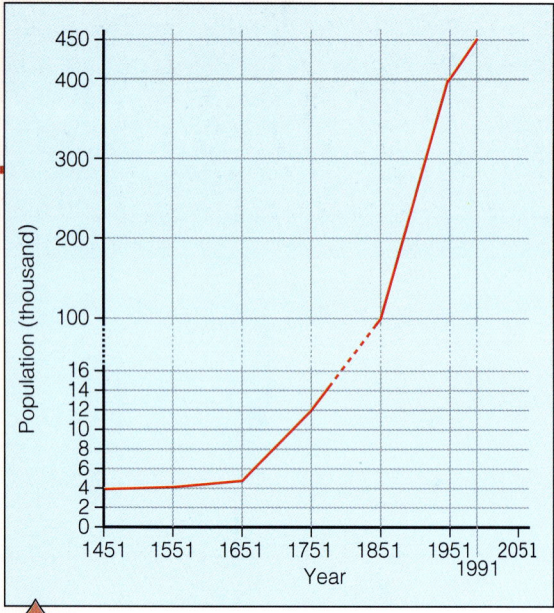

A The growth of Greater Nottingham

Wollaton Hall Nottingham: built with money earned from the sale of local coal.

Nottingham grew as a trading centre: Barges could travel from the sea along the River Trent to Nottingham.

Cotton factories used water from local rivers and horses to power their machines.

B The changing functions of Nottingham

1 Look at GRAPH **A**.
  a What was the population of Nottingham in
    • 1451 • 1751 • 1951 • 1991?
  b Copy and complete this passage by choosing the correct words from each pair.

Between 1451 and 1651 the population of Nottingham changed a great deal/very little. From 1651 to 1951 it rose/fell very slowly/quickly. Since then the change has still been downwards/upwards but at a much slower/faster rate.

SETTLEMENT 3

Local coal was first used in the factories in 1851. Nottingham grew as a hosiery centre.

Cheaper imports from abroad caused many factories to close. Other factories moved to new sites and used larger machines and fewer people.

By 1885 there were 2250 lace-making machines in Nottingham.

800 — 1850 — 1900 — 1950 — 2000

New industries like Raleigh bikes and Boots the chemists grew alongside the textile factories.

Old factories are put to new uses: Nottingham University expands by rebuilding the old Raleigh factory.

There are serious unemployment problems in many parts of the city.

2 Look at TIMELINE **B**.
  a Make a list of jobs done by the people of Nottingham up to 1960.
  b Explain why jobs in Nottingham have changed with time.

3 a What power did Nottingham factories use in the late 18th century?
  b How had this changed by the late 19th century?
  c How does TIMELINE **B** suggest that Nottingham's location helped it stay as an important centre as these changes took place?

4 Suggest why the population of Nottingham has grown in the last 300 years.

5 a What has caused jobs to decline in the late 20th century?
  b Suggest what effect this may have on the population size.

6 Suggest how Nottingham may want its functions to develop in the future. Explain your decision.

4 Service with a smile

What are services?
How are services provided?
Are we all being served?

Wherever we live, we rely on services. They can help to make our lives more healthy, safe, pleasant and easy. Some services, like electricity, are linked to our homes. Others are brought to us, while we must travel to reach some services like shops.

A Delhi: a public telephone helps contact other parts of the world

B Nottingham: television broadcasts come directly into our homes

1 List the services being provided in PHOTOS **A**, **B** and **C**.

2 a Make a table like the one below.

Service	Linked to home	Brought to home	Travel to reach
Television	✓		
Window cleaner		✓	

b Discuss other services and add them to your table.

c Which of the services you have listed:
• keep you safe • keep you healthy • make life more pleasant • make life easier?

3 Explain what is meant by the word 'service'.

C Trams in Hong Kong. We rely on transport services.

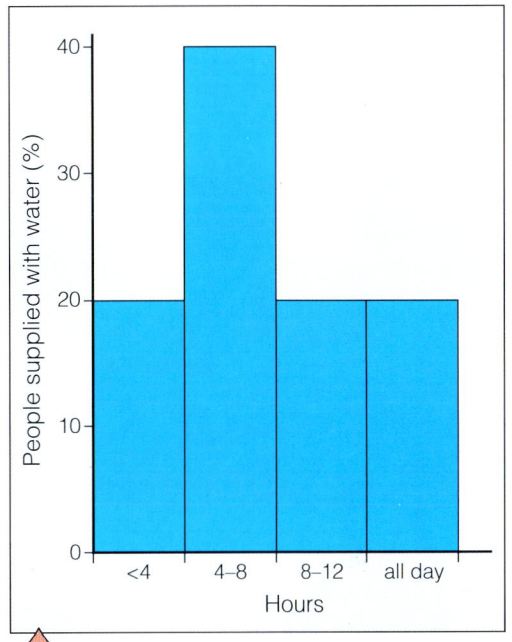

D Water supply in Delhi

> The village is very peaceful. Our cottage has views over the surrounding countryside. We love living in Stowe. Because Stowe is a village, though, away from main towns, we are not linked to all services. We did not have gas here until recently. It was always thought too expensive to connect us. There are no mains sewers to most of the village, and all our sewage goes into a <u>septic tank</u> at the bottom of our garden.

E What services reach Stowe-by-Chartley Staffordshire, UK?

4 Look at GRAPH **D**.
  a What percentage of people in Delhi have water all the time?
  b What percentage have water for less than 8 hours each day?
  c How does this compare with your own area?

5 Look at PHOTO **E**.
  a What does the person think about living in Stowe-by-Chartley?
  b What service does he say is not provided in the village?
  c Suggest how this may affect his life.

6 Make a list of the five services you might need most. Compare your list with others in your class.

7 Describe how well your area is served. How does its services compare with Stowe-by-Chartley?

5 | Shopping in France

How far do people travel for shops and other services?
Why do some settlements have more services than others?

Goods we buy may be divided into convenience goods and comparison goods.

Convenience goods are bought often. They are usually cheap and people want to reach them easily. People travel mainly short distances to buy them.

Comparison goods are not bought very often. They usually cost a lot of money and people like to compare them before buying. People are willing to travel longer distances to buy comparison goods.

A Convenience goods and comparison goods

1 a Describe what is meant by a convenience good.
 b Make a list of convenience goods shown on this page.
 c Add other convenience goods to your list.

2 a Describe what is meant by comparison goods.
 b Make a list of comparison goods found on this page.
 c Add other comparison goods to your list.

3 Compare your lists with others in your group.

SETTLEMENT 5

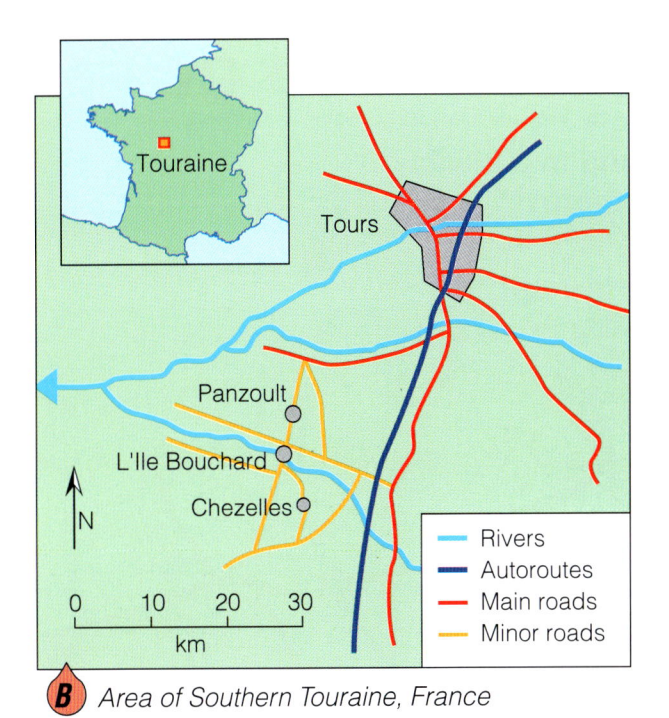

Whether shops and services are close by depends upon where people live. If you can get to shops and services easily, they are <u>accessible</u>. If they are difficult to reach they are <u>inaccessible</u>.

B Area of Southern Touraine, France

C L' Ile Bouchard

D <u>Superstore</u>, Tours

Settlement	Chezelles	Tours	Panzoult	L'Ile Bouchard
Population	50	100 000+	1000	10 000
Church	✓	✓	✓	✓
Public phone	✓	✓	✓	✓
Post box	✓	✓	✓	✓
Post office		Poste		Poste
Cafe/Bar		✓	✓	✓
Baker		✓	✓	✓
Bank		✓		✓
Department store		✓		
Clothes shop		✓		✓

E Population and service details

4 Use MAP **B** to describe the location of Touraine.

5 a Describe the shop shown in PHOTO **C**.
  b Is it likely to sell convenience goods, comparison goods or both?

6 a Describe the shop shown in PHOTO **D**.
  b Is it likely to sell convenience goods, comparison goods or both?

7 a Look at SOURCE **E**. Place the settlements in rank order according to the range of services they provide.
  b Look at the population figures. What do you notice about your lists?

8 a Where might a person living in Chezelles travel:
  • to post a letter • to visit a clothes shop
  • to buy a washing machine?
  b How far would the person travel in each case?
  c How accessible are these services in your own area?

15

6 | Shopping around ... the city

**What different shopping areas are found in a city?
How do these serve the people living there?
Where does my family shop?**

In and around any city there are many shopping areas. These range from very large to very small. The goods and services they sell usually depends upon their <u>location</u> and the number of people who are in their <u>catchment area</u>.

A Nottingham city centre

Nuthall

Aspley

B <u>Retail park</u>

C Shopping parade for a housing estate

D Main road shopping parade

1 *Use* KEY **H** *to complete a copy of the table below. List each of the shopping centres shown in* PHOTOS **B** *to* **G**. *Place them in order according to how near the city centre they are. List the closest first.* **G** *has been done for you.*

Centre description	Location	Types of goods	Means of travel	Average distance travelled
Shopping arcade	In the Central Business District in the middle of Nottingham. Close to a bus station.	Convenience Comparison	Car Bus Other	More than 6 kilometres

6 SETTLEMENT

H Key to shopping habits

Types of goods:	🛒 convenience	🌿 comparison
Travel to shops:	🚶 walk 🚗 car 🚌 bus ↔ other
Average distance travelled:	2 4 6 <2 km	2 4 6 4–6 km
	2 4 6 2–4 km	2 4 6 >6 km

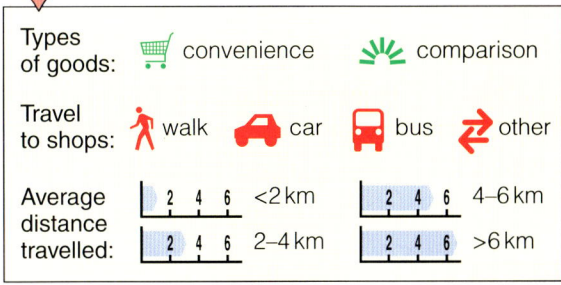

E Inner city supermarket

🛒 🚶 🚗 🚌   2 4 6

F Corner shop

🛒 🚶   2 4 6

G Shopping arcade in the Central Business District (CBD)

🛒 🌿 🚗 🚌 ↔   2 4 6

Map: Nottingham, New Basford, City centre. Scale 0–1 km, N.

---

2 a Place the shopping centres in rank order according to the distance people travel to them.

b What link is there between the distance people travel and how they travel to the shopping centre?

c Explain the link you have described.

3 a Suggest a group of people who may prefer to shop for convenience goods in the city centre. Explain your choice.

b Suggest a group of people who may find shopping in the city centre very difficult. Explain your choice.

4 Do a survey of the shopping habits of members of your family. Find out:
- how often they use different types of shops
- how they travel to these shops
- how far they travel.

Compare your results with other members of your class.

17

7 | Shopping changes

How are shopping locations changing?
How do these changes affect people?

Many corner shops have closed down. Others have changed the goods they sell. They find it difficult to compete with superstores and large retail parks. What do corner shops offer people? Why have so many closed? Some of the new superstores are built close to city centres where the corner shops once were. Others are in out-of-town locations where land prices are cheaper and there is more land for car-parks.

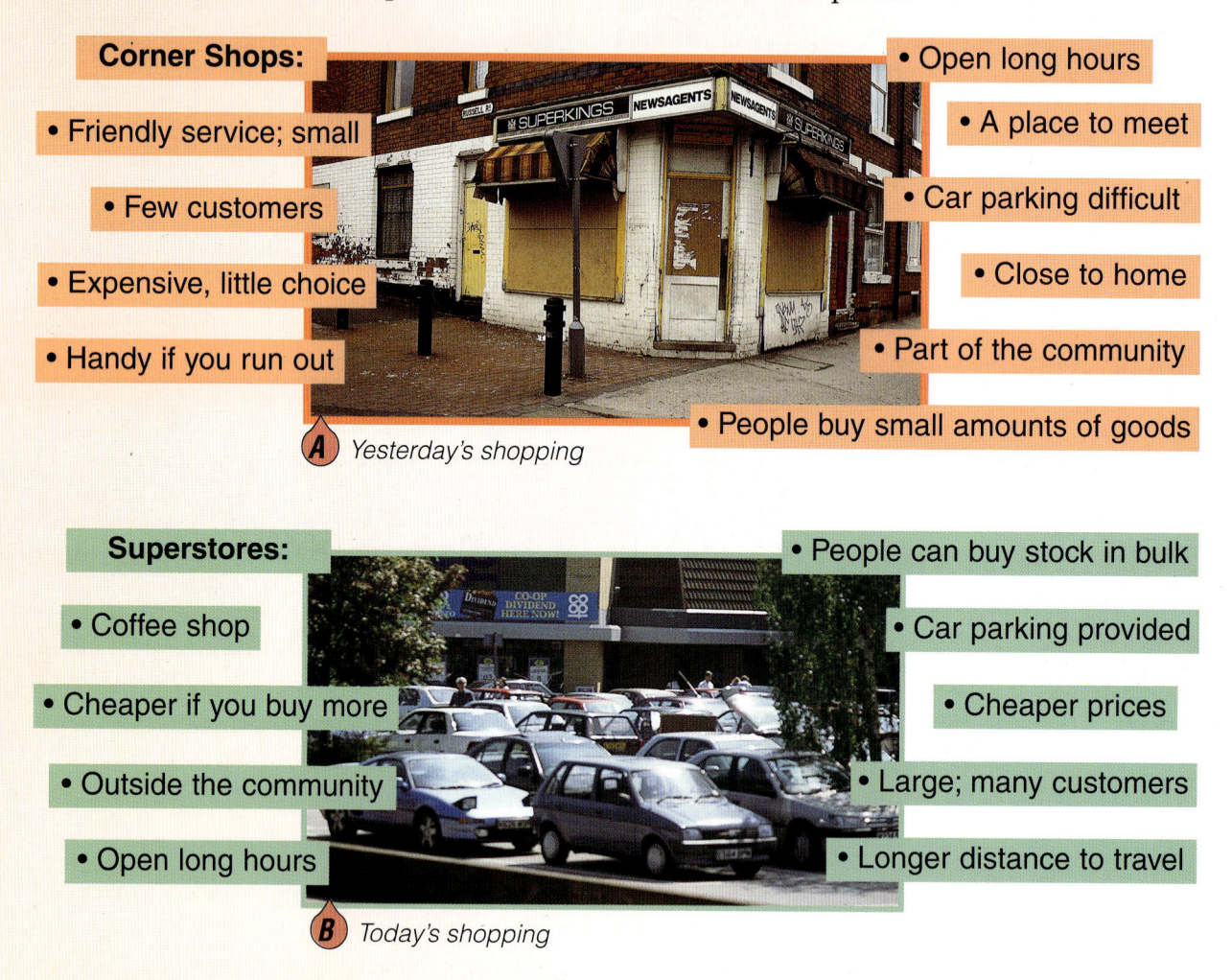

Corner Shops:
- Friendly service; small
- Few customers
- Expensive, little choice
- Handy if you run out
- Open long hours
- A place to meet
- Car parking difficult
- Close to home
- Part of the community
- People buy small amounts of goods

A *Yesterday's shopping*

Superstores:
- Coffee shop
- Cheaper if you buy more
- Outside the community
- Open long hours
- People can buy stock in bulk
- Car parking provided
- Cheaper prices
- Large; many customers
- Longer distance to travel

B *Today's shopping*

---

1 *Look at* PHOTO **A**.
  a *Using just the photo, list five words which describe the corner shop.*
  b *Describe the service that corner shops provide for local people.*
  c *Explain why some corner shops are closing.*

2 *Look at* PHOTO **B** *and the words around it.*
  a *Describe the superstore. Use these headings:*
     • *size* • *space* • *position* • *facilities.*
  b *Explain why superstores are popular with many shoppers.*

C Fred Stubbs and the superstore

Anna Franklin
Age: 24
Occupation: Local government officer
Salary: £15 000

Jermaine Franklin
Age: 26
Occupation: Motor mechanic
Salary: £14 000

Other details about the Franklins
Home: semi-detached house on the edge of town
Family: no children yet
Transport: a small family hatchback

D Personal profile: the Franklins

3 Look at STORYBOARD **C**.
  a Discuss Fred's journey. Make a list of the problems he faced.
  b Explain why Fred is likely to prefer using his corner shop.
  c Suggest what superstores can do to help people like Fred.

4 What other groups of people may have problems in a superstore? Describe the difficulties they may have.

5 Look at PROFILE **D**.
  a List the facts about the Franklins that make shopping at a superstore a good idea for them.
  b Make a storyboard to describe a journey to the superstore by the Franklins.

6 What do you think about the changes that are taking place in how people shop?

8 | The changing village

What is a village?
How do villages change with time?
How do the changes affect the villagers?

Stowe-by-Chartley is a village of 457 people. It is located in the county of Staffordshire in the West Midlands region of England. It has seen many changes during the last 75 years. The jobs that its inhabitants do have changed. The size of its built up area has altered and the services it provides have also changed.

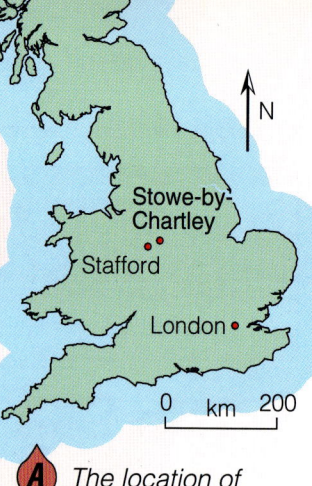

A The location of Stowe-by-Chartley

1920
Many inhabitants worked in farming.
Other jobs, which no longer exist, included wheelwright, farrier, blacksmith, carpenter, butler, station-master and crossing-gate keeper.

1991
Managerial and technical (60%)
e.g. engineers, town planners
Skilled manual (30%)
e.g. farmworkers, healthcarers
Skilled non-manual (10%)
e.g. bank clerks, teachers

C Jobs in Stowe-by-Chartley, 1920 and 1991

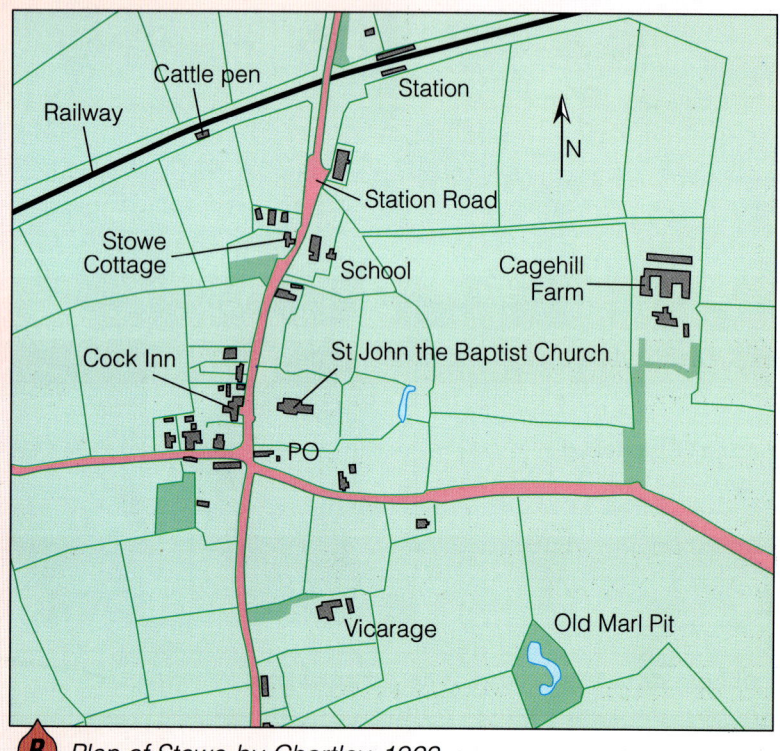

B Plan of Stowe-by-Chartley, 1923

---

1 a Use MAP **A** and an atlas to describe the location of Stowe-by-Chartley.

2 Look at PLAN **B**.
  a Which of the following services are shown:
    • inn • bus station • church • railway station • hairdresser?
  b Name another service shown on PLAN **B**.
  c Suggest why some other services might have been found in the village but not shown on the map.

3 Study TABLE **C**.
  a A farrier is a person who puts new shoes on horses. Discuss what is meant by each of the other jobs done in the village in the 1920s. Write a definition of each job.
  b Choose two of these jobs and explain why they are not found in the village now.

4 a Write a sentence to describe the types of jobs done by people who now live in the village.
  b How have the jobs done by people living in Stowe-by-Chartley changed?

SETTLEMENT 8

OLD **NEW**

E *Old and new houses in Stowe-by-Chartley*

D *Plan of Stowe-by-Chartley, 1997*

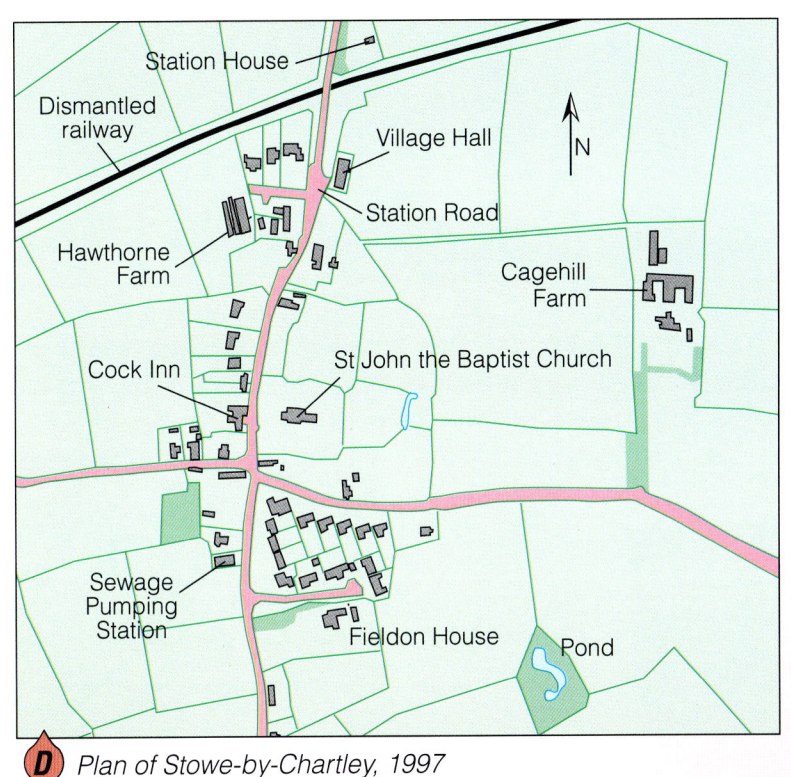

F *The people of Stowe-by-Chartley hold a village fête every June*

5 a On a copy of PLAN **B**, mark the changes shown on PLAN **D**. You should include:
- buildings that have changed their use
- buildings that have been added
- services that have changed.

6 a Look at PHOTO **E**. Compare the old and new houses. Include information on size, style and building materials.
b How well do the new houses appear to fit into the village?

7 Look at PHOTO **F**.
a Describe the activities in the photo.
b Make a list of the activities you might have in a village fête. Remember there will be all ages of people at the fête.
c Suggest why many people in Stowe-by-Chartley think the fête is an important part of village life.

8 Why is Stowe-by-Chartley described as a village?

21

9 Getting around

How do people in villages travel?
How has their means of travel changed?
How do these changes affect villagers?

The single-track railway line, a branch of the Great Northern Railway, was built shortly after 1900. It wound its way from Stafford to Uttoxeter, stopping five times… The station, situated just beside the bridge in Stowe, was a busy loading point for milk, cattle, coal and salt, as well as passengers. The track was eventually taken away in 1956.

A Stowe-by-Chartley's railway history

	NS	NS	NS	NS	a.m.	Noon	p.m.	p.m.	p.m.	p.m.	p.m.	p.m.	SS	p.m.	SS	SS
Stowe	7 20	8 25	9 25	10 25	11 25	12 25	1 35	2 35	3 35	4 35	5 35	6 35	7 35	8 35	9 35	10 35
Amerton	7 23	8 28	9 28	10 28	11 28	12 28	1 38	2 38	3 38	4 38	5 38	6 38	7 38	8 38	9 38	10 38
Weston	7 28	8 33	9 33	10 33	11 33	12 33	1 43	2 43	3 43	4 43	5 43	6 43	7 43	8 43	9 43	10 43
Stafford arr.	7 45	8 50	9 50	10 50	11 50	12 50	2 00	3 00	4 00	5 00	6 00	7 00	8 00	9 00	10 00	11 00

NS–Not Sundays. SS–Saturdays and Sundays only

B Stowe's bus service in 1954.
There was also a similar return timetable.

1 Look at EXTRACT **A**.
  a Between which two towns did the trains travel?
  b List the goods they carried.
  c Suggest two reasons why passengers would go to Stafford.

2 a When did the railway line disappear?
  b Suggest why it closed.
  c Name a group of people who may have been affected by the closure. Explain your choice.

3 Look at TIMETABLE **B**.
  a How frequent was the bus service between Stowe and Stafford?
  b How many buses did not run at the weekend?
  c How many buses ran only at the weekend?
  d Explain why weekday and weekend services were different.
  e Suggest why a frequent bus service was important to the villagers in the 1950s.

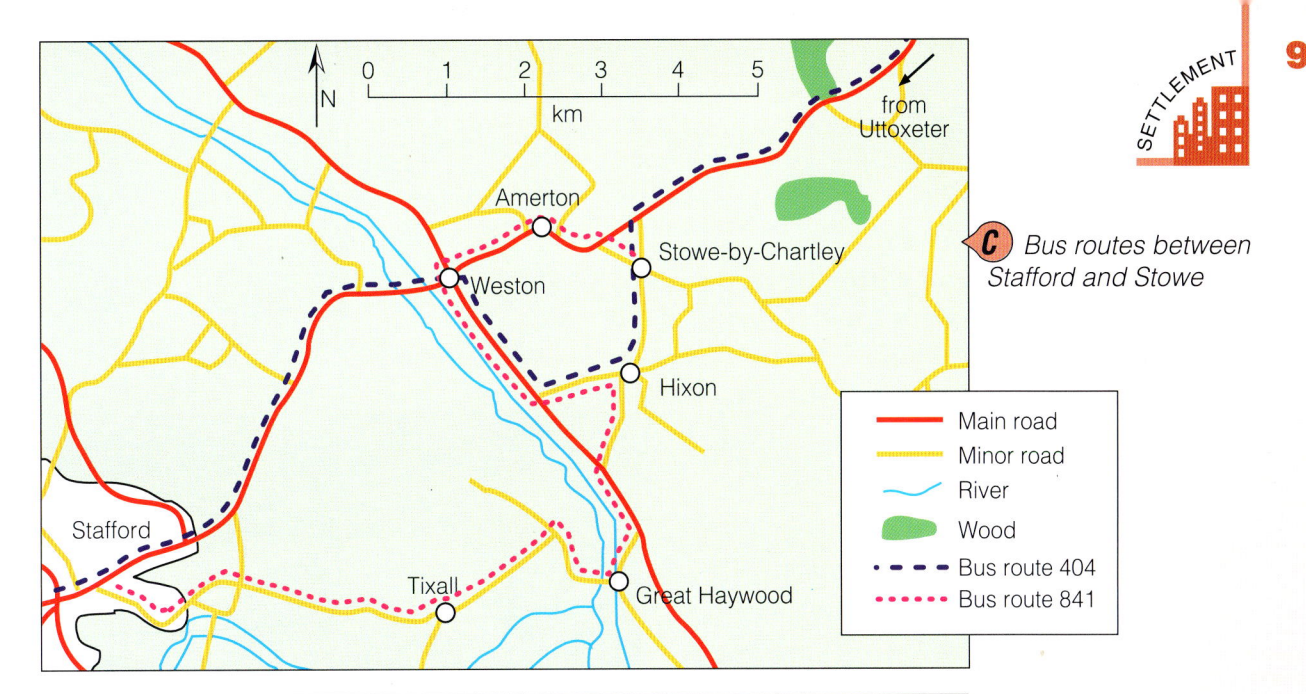

SETTLEMENT 9

C Bus routes between Stafford and Stowe

Stowe depart	7:59	9:59	11:59	14:13	16:13	17:13	*18:35	*21:47
Stafford arrive	8:25	10:25	12:25	14:40	16:40	17:40	19:10	22:19
Stafford depart	8:35	10:30	12:30	14:40	16:40	17:40	*18:15	*21:15	*22:30
Stowe arrive	9:00	10:55	12:55	15:05	17:05	18:05	18:50	21:47	23:02

*Route 841 All other times Route 404

D Stowe's bus service in 1997. There is no Sunday bus service. (The bus routes are <u>subsidised</u> by Staffordshire County Council.)

Household car ownership: no car 11.6%, one car 42.2%, two or more cars 46.2%

Transport to work: train 5%, bus 5%, motor-cycle 5%, by foot 5%, work at home 15%, car 65%

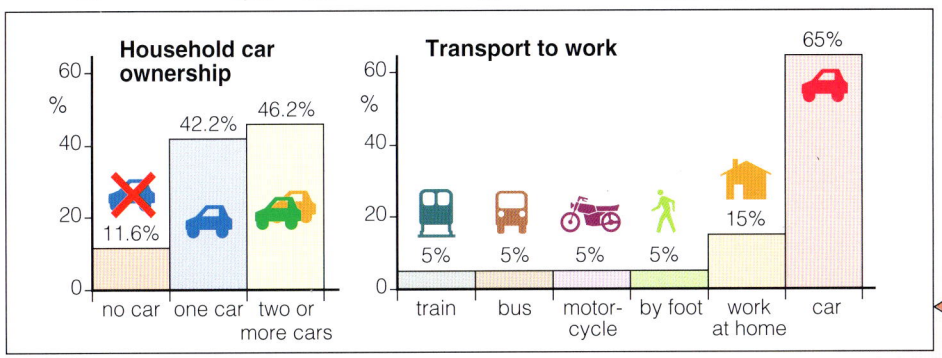

E 1991 <u>census</u> details for Stowe

4 Look at MAP **C**.
   a Describe the route taken by the 404 bus from Stowe to Stafford.
   b How is the 841 route different from this?
   c Explain why the bus does not take the most direct route between Stowe and Stafford.

5 Look at TIMETABLE **D**.
   a Which buses may be used by these people:
   • a pupil at a Stafford secondary school
   • a spectator at Stafford Rangers Football Club
   • people going to a Stafford night club.
   b Would there be any travel problems for any of these groups of people?
   c Is the bus service of 1997 better or poorer than that of 1954? Explain your answer.

6 Look at CENSUS **E**. Explain as fully as possible why many of the residents of Stowe-by-Chartley do not need to rely on the bus service.

7 a Name a group of people who may need the bus service. Explain your choice.
   b Suggest what would happen if Staffordshire County Council no longer subsidised the bus service.
   c Design a poster to persuade the bus company to keep this village service open.

23

10 Using the land

How do we use land?
How does land use differ from place to place?
How can we map the use of land?

1 Industry is to do with people working and earning a living.

A A train at Delhi Railway Station

2 Places of worship are where people go to praise their god.

B A cycle road race. in Panzoult, France

3 Recreation takes place in our spare time. It is how we enjoy ourselves.

A residential area of Delhi, India C

24

10 SETTLEMENT

D Building new offices, Hong Kong

E Nathan Road, central Hong Kong

4 Shops sell us many of the articles we need to live our lives.

5 Transport helps us to move from place to place.

6 Housing gives us the shelter we need.

F The Sikh Golden Temple, Amritsar, India

1 *Look at the information on these pages. For each boxed sentence:*
 a *Copy the sentence.*
 b *Write a short description of the photo that matches the sentence.*
 c *Suggest other examples of this type of land use. One has been done for you below.*

> Recreation takes place in our spare time. It is how we enjoy ourselves.
> Photo B shows young people taking part in a cycle road race. It is in the village of Panzoult in France.
> Other ways in which land is used for recreation includes football and hockey pitches, swimming pools, cinemas, bingo halls, bowling alleys and ice rinks.

2 *Use a copy of* PLAN **D** *on page 21 and this key to make a land-use survey of Stowe-by-Chartley in 1997.*

Colour code	Land use
	Industry
	Transport
	Housing
	Recreation
	Place of worship
	Shops
	Other

3 a *Do a similar survey for the area around your school.*
 b *Draw sketches or take photos to show the different types of land use.*

4 *Describe how the land use around your home compares with that of Stowe-by-Chartley.*

25

11 | Land use in a city

How is land used in Nottingham?
How do different parts of the city compare?
What patterns of land use exist?

All cities have a number of things in common. They have large areas of houses to shelter their people. They also have shops and offices. These provide services for people. Schools and colleges also give a service. Many people living in a city are employed in the industries found there.

1 PHOTOS **A–E** are of places in each of the following grid squares on MAP **G**:
• 5445 • 5639 • 5436 • 5737 • 5438.

Complete a copy of the table by matching the grid square with a description of the photo:

Grid square	Photo
5737	Pupils leaving a secondary school at the end of the day
5639	

2 The Central Business District (CBD) of Nottingham is in grid squares 5739 and 5740. Use evidence from MAP **G** and PHOTO **F** to complete this description of the CBD:
The CBD is in the middle/at the edge of the city. It is a place that has few/many large shops and offices. It is a centre of main _____ and there is both a _____ and _____ station nearby. Tourists could be helped at the _____ office and there is both a _____ and a _____ for them to visit.

26

Market Square in the centre of Nottingham's CBD

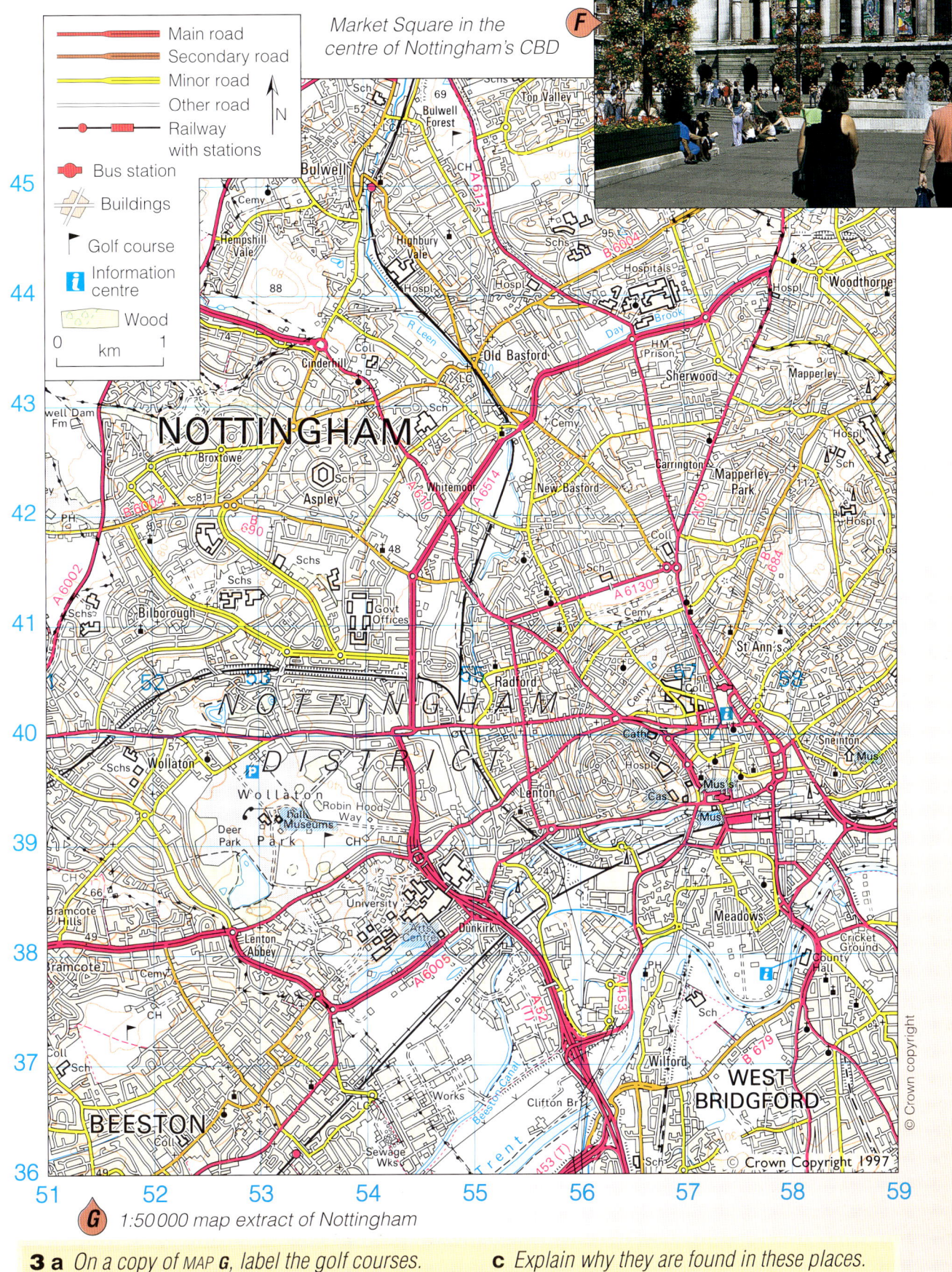

G 1:50 000 map extract of Nottingham

3 a On a copy of MAP **G**, label the golf courses.
b What is the direction and distance of each course from the city centre (5739)?
c Explain why they are found in these places.

4 Suggest types of leisure uses found in the city centre. Explain your choices.

27

12 Living in the city

How does housing differ around a city?
How does housing affect people's quality of life?
How is housing changing?

Where people live affects their quality of life. Figures used in the census can help to measure quality of life. We can also look at an area in which people live and form our own opinions as to how pleasant that area appears. Perhaps, though, it may be better to ask the people who live there what they think.

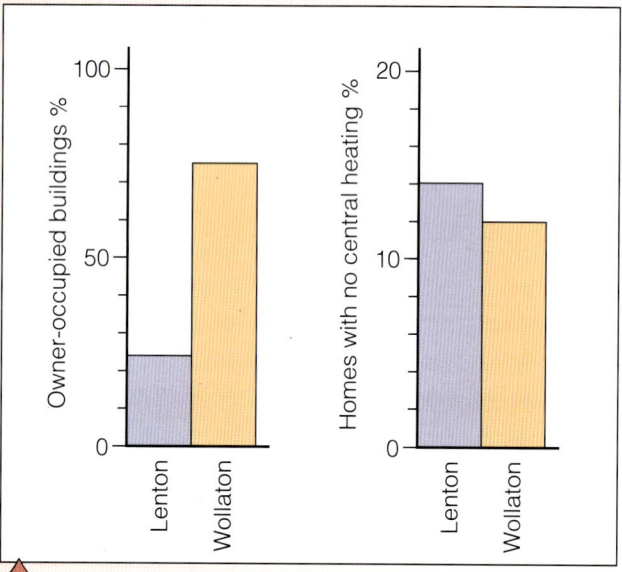

C 1991 census information for Lenton and Wollaton wards

B Terraced housing and high-rise flats in Lenton

D Thinking about Lenton

> I've lived here all my life. The neighbours are great. We are a very close community and always help each other. The bus stop is just round the corner and I can be in town in just five minutes. Move from here? Never.

1 Use MAP A to complete the following sentence:
Lenton is located about two/ten kilometres east/west of Nottingham city centre.

2 Study PHOTO B.
   a Write five words which describe the area of the photo.
   b Use your words to make a sentence which describes these Lenton houses.

3 Look at GRAPHS C and F.
   a Describe what the graphs tell you about housing in Lenton.
   b What do the graphs suggest about people's quality of life?

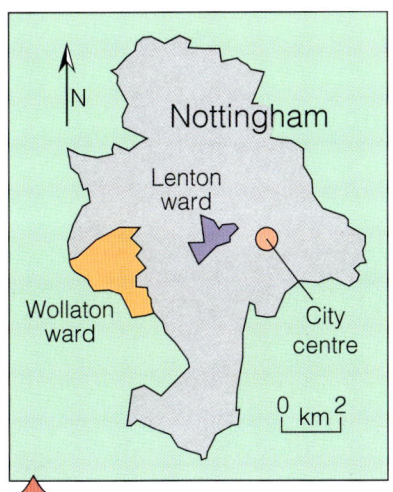

SETTLEMENT 12

A Location of two Nottingham wards

E Detached houses in Wollaton

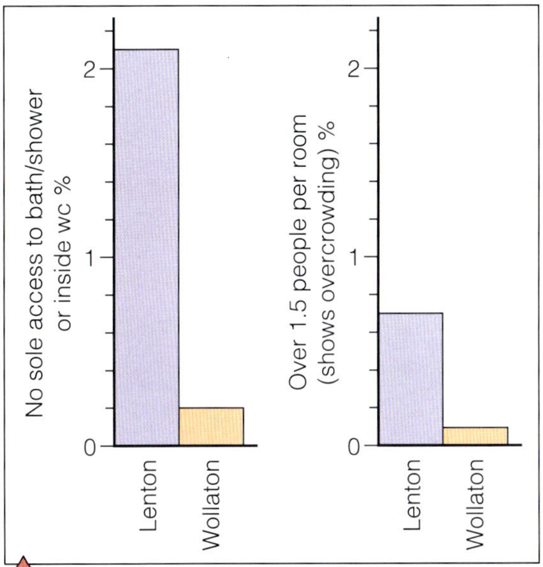

F 1991 census information for Lenton and Wollaton wards

> We moved here last year. It isn't easy to make friends; no one ever seems to be in. If I haven't got the car, getting around is quite difficult. It's a long walk to the bus stop, and the buses are not very frequent.

G Thinking about Wollaton

H Many parts of the inner city are being rebuilt

4 Use MAP **A** to describe the location of Wollaton.

5 Write a sentence to describe the houses in PHOTO **E**.

6 Look at GRAPHS **C** and **F**.
  a Describe what the graphs tell you about housing in Wollaton.
  b What do the graphs suggest about people's quality of life?

7 Look at THOUGHT BUBBLE **G** and other information on these pages. Would you prefer to live in Lenton or Wollaton? Explain your choice.

8 Using information on these pages, suggest how useful is census information for telling us about people's quality of life?

13 | Changing patterns

**What patterns of council housing exist in Nottingham?
How have council housing patterns changed in recent years?
In what other ways is Nottingham changing today?**

From 1900 until 1981 local councils built houses. Many are still rented to the people who live in them. Some of these houses were built in <u>suburbs</u> to rehouse people who lived close to the city centre. Others were built on land where old houses had been knocked down. Most of these were in, or near, the <u>inner city</u>.

Flats knocked down
1960s council flats at Balloon Woods, Hyson Green and Basford are to be demolished after less than 30 years of use. The flats have been described as a disgrace by residents. They suffer from damp, vandalism and crime.

B *Council flats demolished*

Victorian terraces replaced
St Ann's and the Meadows had some of the poorest housing in Nottingham. Most houses had no indoor WC and many didn't have a bath. These have now been replaced by town houses and flats which offer facilities the residents could only have dreamed about a couple of years ago.

C *New buildings*

A *The growth of council housing in Nottingham*

Map legend:
- Estates built 1919–1939
- Estates built 1945–1969
- Estates built 1970–1983
- Small groups of houses and flats built 1919–1983
- City boundary

1 a Describe what is meant by a council house.
  b Give two reasons why councils built houses.

2 a Use MAP A to complete the following passage:
  Most of the council estates built between 1945 and 1969 were in the inner city/suburbs. Those found to the west of the city centre include S_____ , B_____ and B_____ W_____ . Bestwood is found to the _____ and _____ to the south of the city centre. Those which are near/away from the city centre include Hyson Green, _____ and _____ .

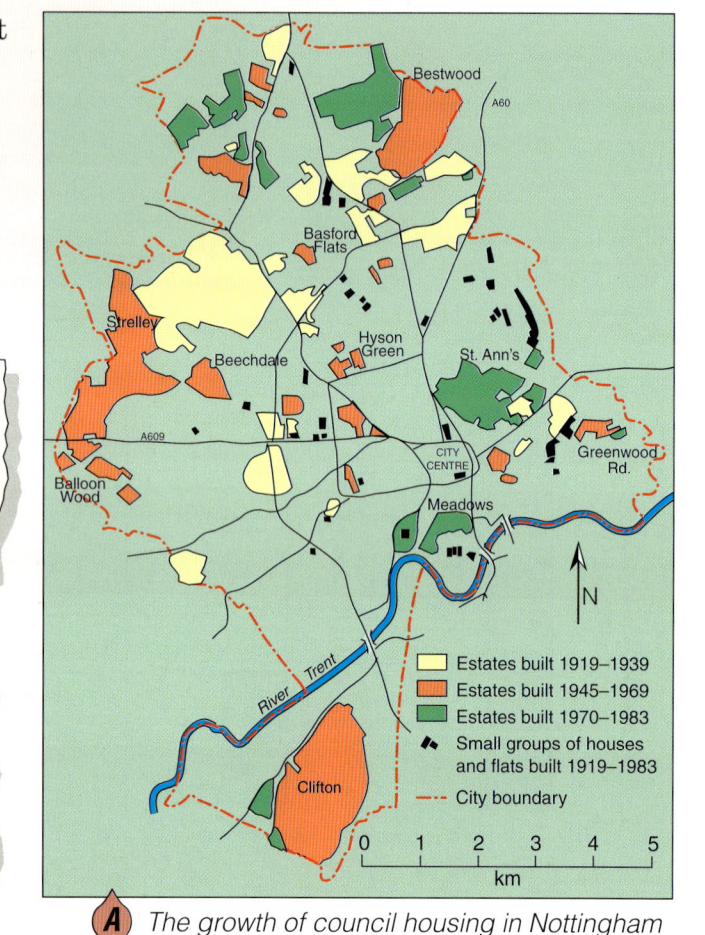

  b Describe the distribution of council houses built between 1970 and 1983.
  c Roughly how much of Nottingham is covered by council housing: 10%, 30%, 50% or 70%?
  d Discuss other ways in which houses may be owned.

3 Look at MAP A and ARTICLE B.
  a Describe the location of Balloon Woods flats.
  b When were these flats built?
  c When were they knocked down? Why?

Changing cities

Cities are always changing. New buildings replace old ones. City areas are now much greater than their official boundaries because new houses are being built in the suburbs. Old areas, in the inner city, are being redeveloped. Also, the way people travel is changing as people become concerned about traffic jams and pollution from cars.

D *Building in the south-west suburbs of Nottingham, 1997*

E *Lottery money is used to help build Nottingham's new ice stadium, with two indoor and one outdoor rinks*

F *An old industrial route provides leisure opportunities for people living in inner Nottingham*

G *Nottingham follows Manchester and Sheffield with plans for a new Light Rapid Transit System* (Adtranz Eurotram)

4 Look at ARTICLE **C**.
  a What problems did residents of St Ann's and the Meadows face before their houses were replaced?
  b Suggest how the new houses may have affected the lives of the people living there.
  c Imagine you lived in a slum house with few modern facilities. Discuss which you would prefer. To be rehoused on the edge of the city or to have new houses built where you live in the inner city?

5 Look at PHOTOS **D** to **G**.
  a Suggest how each change is likely to affect the lives of people living in Nottingham.
  b Write a letter to your local newspaper describing the changes you would like to see in your village or local town or city. Explain why you would like these changes.

14 | The growing city

Where is Delhi?
How quickly is Delhi growing?
How does Delhi provide for people's needs?

A Location of Delhi

Delhi is the capital city of India. People have lived there for over 3000 years. Now it is one of the world's fastest growing cities.

B Delhi is a very busy city

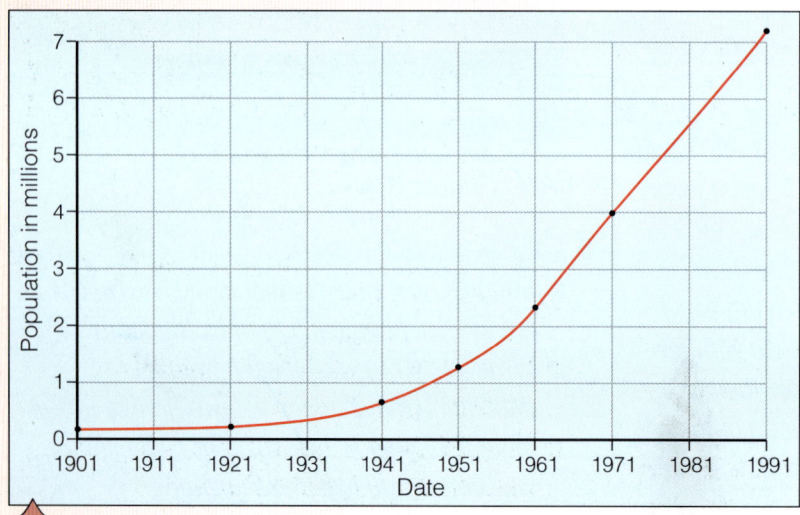

C Delhi's population is expected to double every 18 years

1 Describe the location of Delhi. Use MAP **A** and an atlas to help you.

2 Look at PHOTO **B**.
  a Write five words which best describe the scene.
  b Use these words to help you write two or three sentences to describe a street scene in Delhi.

3 Look at GRAPH **C**.
  a What was the population of Delhi in 1901?
  b What was its population in 1991?
  c Compare the rate at which Delhi grew before and after 1941.

32

SETTLEMENT 14

D *Different types of houses*

People need shelter, food and water. It is difficult to provide these in a city growing as fast as Delhi. A place to live may not be easy to find and will be expensive to buy or rent. Many people live in slums or on the street. The supply of clean water is also a problem. One in five people have access to tap-water for *less than* four hours a day. Finding space to play can also be difficult for children.

E *Essential services: water is often sold on the streets from large containers*

F *Play time: space for games is sometimes not easy to find*

4 Look at the houses in PHOTOS **D**.
 a List how they are similar.
 b List how they are different.
 c In which house would you prefer to live? Explain why.
 d Suggest the different lifestyles of the people living in these two houses.

5 Look at PHOTOS **E** and **F**. What do they tell you about life in Delhi?

6 a Using GRAPH **C**, estimate the population of Delhi for the year 2009.
 b Suggest how such growth may affect the lives of people living in the city.

33

Settlement glossary

Accessible
When it is easy to get to a place, or use a service.

Boundary
A line that separates an area from another area.

Bridging point
A stretch of river where a bridge could be built across. Roads often come together at bridging points.

Capital city
The city which has the national government offices of that country.

Capital cities

Catchment area
The area from where a service draws the people who want to use it, e.g. a school takes its pupils from a certain area, or a shop its customers.

Census
A count of all the people in a country. It usually includes information about their houses and the jobs they do.

Central Business District (CBD)
The area in the middle of a city where many shops and offices are found.

Function
The purpose, or main activity, of a settlement. A town is often described by its main function. For example, Blackpool is a holiday resort.

Blackpool beach

House
Terraced: one of a number of houses joined together in a row.

Semi-detached: one of a pair of houses joined together.

Detached: a house on its own.

34

Inaccessible
When it is difficult to get to a place, or use a service.

Inhabitants
People who live in a certain place.

Inner city
The area surrounding the **CBD**. Here, many old houses and factories may have been replaced or are being replaced.
The inner city is different from the **suburbs**.

Location
The position where places are found on the Earth. For example, where services are placed in settlements.

Nomads
People who move from place to place and have no permanent home.

Offices
Places where business is carried out.

Quality of life
A measure of how content people are with their lives and their surroundings.

Region
An area with definite boundaries for a **function** or purpose. For example, the UK can be divided into television or standard regions.

The UK: standard regions

SCOTLAND
NORTHERN IRELAND
NORTH EAST
NORTH WEST
YORKSHIRE & HUMBER
MERSEYSIDE
EAST MIDLANDS
WEST MIDLANDS
EASTERN
WALES
LONDON
SOUTH WEST
SOUTH EAST

Retail park
A purpose-built collection of large shops selling different products and sharing a large car park.

Septic tank
A large underground container in which toilet waste is collected.

Shopping arcade
A planned group of shops which are closed in, and so are protected from the weather.

Subsidise
To give part of the cost of something. For example, Staffordshire County Council helps pay for part of the bus service to Stowe-by-Chartley.

Suburbs
The outer parts of a town or city. Inner and outer suburbs are always outside the **inner city** and the **CBD**.

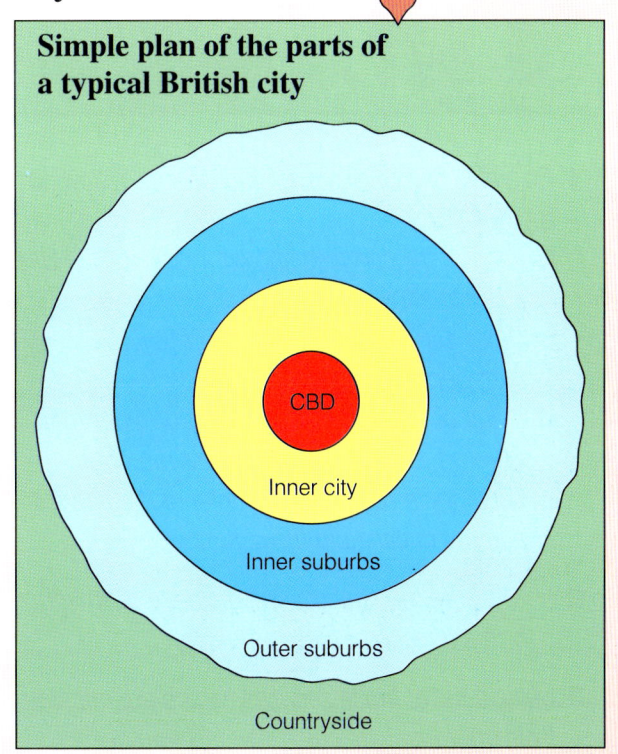

Simple plan of the parts of a typical British city

CBD
Inner city
Inner suburbs
Outer suburbs
Countryside

Superstore
A large supermarket which often has extra services, like a coffee shop or a bank.

The next step is yours...

How well is your area served? How accessible are the services that you need for your life? How easily can you use those services which make your life more enjoyable? Are there any improvements you would wish to make to your area?

A Different services

Secondary school

Petrol station

Doctor's surgery

Newsagent

1 On a map of your area mark and label the following:
   a Your home.
   b Each of the services shown in SERVICES **A**. Use a key to show them.
   c Other services which are important to members of your family.
   d If any of these services are not on your map draw an arrow pointing in their direction. Label the arrow with the name of the service and the distance to the service.

2 a Measure the straight line distance from your home to each of these services.

3 Make a list of those services, which are missing from your local area, that you feel you need.

4 Do you feel that your home is well served or poorly served? Explain your answer.

Population

Shoppers on Ginza Street, Tokyo, Japan

Settlement in Eskdale, the Lake District, UK

What are the differences between these places?
Why do these differences exist?

1 | Where is everybody?

Where do people live?
Why do some areas have either low or high population densities?
Should we be concerned by rapid population growth?

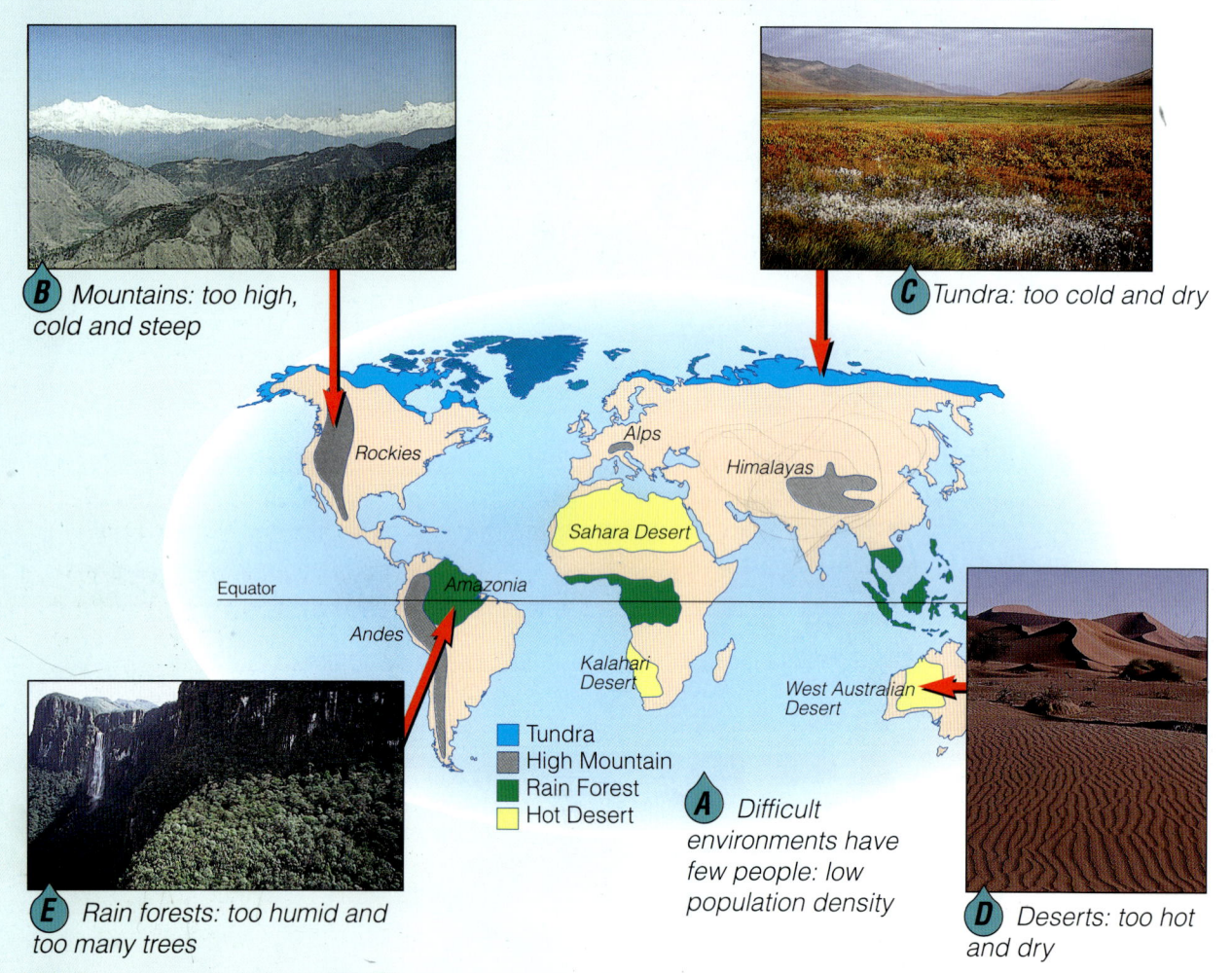

B Mountains: too high, cold and steep

C Tundra: too cold and dry

A Difficult environments have few people: low population density

- Tundra
- High Mountain
- Rain Forest
- Hot Desert

E Rain forests: too humid and too many trees

D Deserts: too hot and dry

Too many people?

Nearly 60 million people live in the United Kingdom (UK). Some live in the countryside but most live in towns and cities. Almost 10 million (1 in every 6 people) live in London. It has a <u>high population density</u> with many people living in a small area.

It is difficult to live in some parts of the world. Places where few people live have a <u>low population density</u>.

There are nearly 6000 million people in the world. But the <u>distribution</u> of where people live is very uneven.

---

1 Study MAP **A** and PHOTOS **B, C, D, E.**
  a On an outline world map shade and label the four difficult environments shown on MAP **A**.
  b Using evidence from the photos, write sentences to suggest why these environments are difficult places for people to live.
  c Choose ONE difficult environment from MAP **A**. Use an atlas to help you describe the location of places with this environment.

Regions with many people: high population density **F**

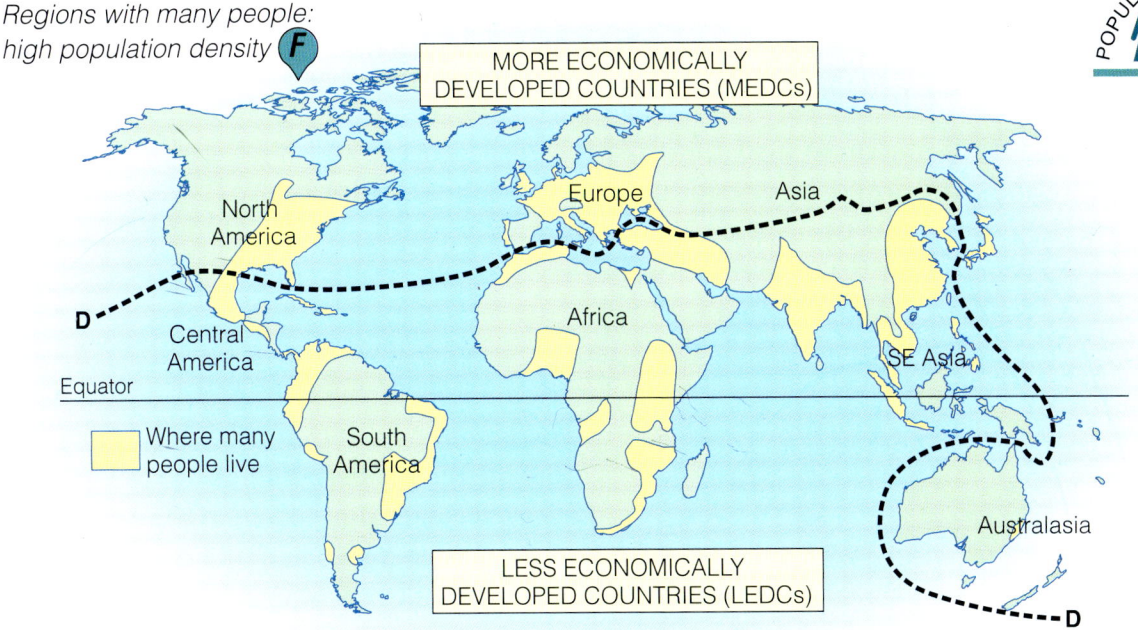

MORE ECONOMICALLY DEVELOPED COUNTRIES (MEDCs)

LESS ECONOMICALLY DEVELOPED COUNTRIES (LEDCs)

Key: Where many people live

Labels on map: North America, Central America, South America, Europe, Africa, Asia, SE Asia, Australasia, Equator, D–D

D–D This line divides the world into More and Less Economically Developed Countries.

- **More Economically Developed Countries** (MEDCs) are countries which have high standards of living and a large share of the world's wealth. They have become wealthy by developing their farming, industries and services.

- **Less Economically Developed Countries** (LEDCs) are countries which have poor standards of living and a small share of the world's wealth. They are trying to increase their wealth by developing farming, industries and services

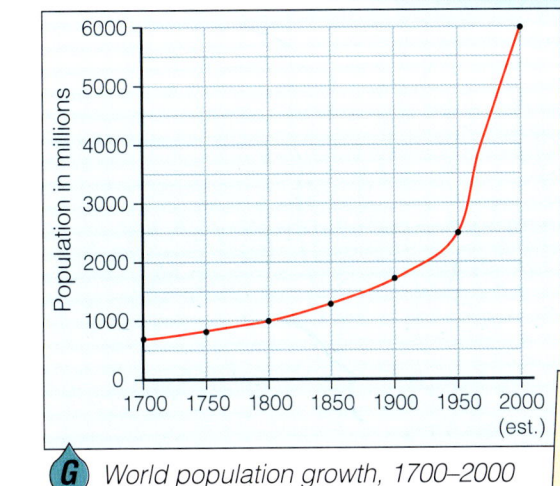

G World population growth, 1700–2000

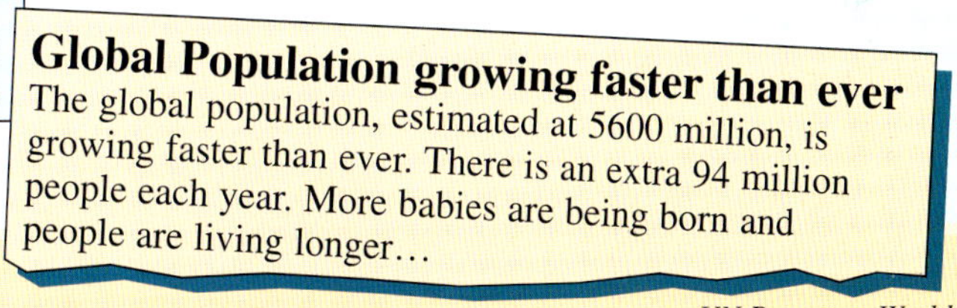

Global Population growing faster than ever

The global population, estimated at 5600 million, is growing faster than ever. There is an extra 94 million people each year. More babies are being born and people are living longer…

UN Report on World Population 1996.

2 Study MAP **F**.
  a On your outline map, shade the regions with many people. Choose your own shading. Add a key.
  b Describe the distribution of regions where many people live.
  c Suggest reasons for the distribution you have described above.

3 Use MAP **F**.
  a What does More Economically Developed Country (MEDC) mean?
  b How is a Less Economically Developed Country (LEDC) different?
  c Using MAP **F** and an atlas, name one MEDC and one LEDC.

4 Look at GRAPH **G**.
  a Copy and complete the following paragraph. The world's population was 1000 million in _____. By 1925 it had reached _____ million, which was _____ the 1800 population. Since 1925 the population took only _____ years to double again to _____ million in 1970. The population will be _____ million by the year 2000.
  b What happens to the number of years it takes to double the population on the graph?

5 Should we be worried about the rate of population growth? Explain your answer.

39

2 | More people are living longer

**Where and why are birth and death rates high and low?
How do these increase or decrease a country's population?
Will having more old people cause problems?**

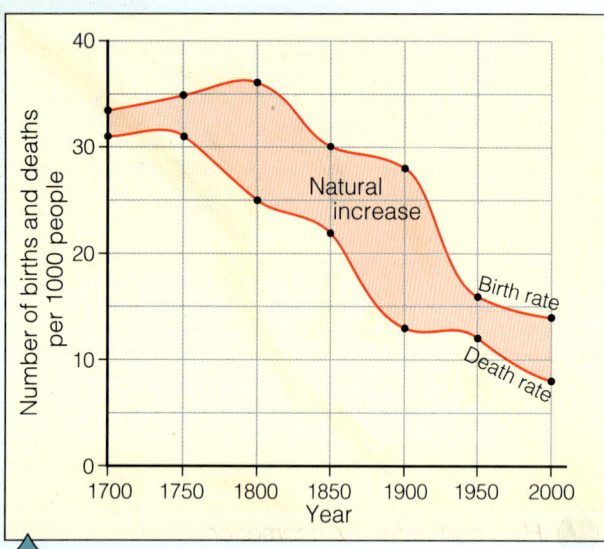

A Birth and death rates in More Economically Developed Countries (MEDCs)

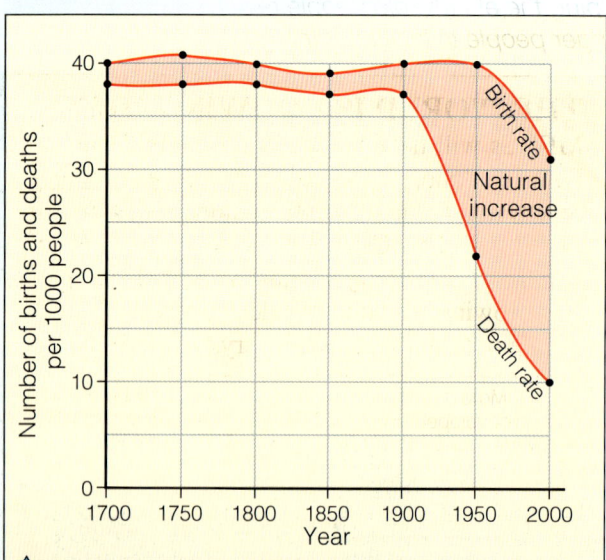

B Birth and death rates in Less Economically Developed Countries (LEDCs)

Birth rate is the number of babies born in a year for every 1000 of the population.

Death rate is the number of people who die in a year for every 1000 of the population.

Too many children?

The global population is estimated at 5600 million. Three babies are born every second. More of them are staying alive. People are also living longer. We can tell this by measuring birth rates and death rates. These vary from 10 (low) to over 30 (high).

The world's population grows when the number of people born is more than the number of people dying. When birth rates are high and death rates are low, the population grows quickly.

1 a How many babies are born each second in the world?
  b Work out how many babies will be born during the time of your lesson.

2 Look at GRAPHS **A** and **B**.
  a Write down five true statements from the list below.
- Death rates come down before birth rates in MEDCs / LEDCs / all countries.
- LEDCs have lower / higher birth rates than MEDCs.
- Death rates and birth rates have fallen rapidly / slowly since 1950 in LEDCs.
- When the birth rate is higher than the death rate, there is a natural increase / natural decrease in population.
- The natural population increase is greater / smaller in MEDCs.

POPULATION 2

C *If many children die young, mothers have lots of babies in the hope that some will survive.*

D *Helping the family income: children work at planting and harvesting.*

E *Helping the elderly: old people rely on younger people to look after them.*

3 Look at PHOTOS **C**, **D** and **E**.
  a What are the advantages of having many children?
  b People have fewer children in most MEDCs. Suggest why.

4 Study the graphs in ARTICLE **F**.
  a How long can people expect to live in MEDCs in the year 2000?
  b How does this compare to the MEDC figure for 1965?
  c Africa is made up of LEDCs. How are these figures different for Africa?

5 a What problems might be caused by having more old people in MEDCs, such as in the UK?
  b How might the problems of population growth be different in LEDCs?

THE WORLD IS GROWING OLDER

MEDCs will have more old people in future. In Europe alone, an increase in <u>life expectancy</u> means that the number of pensioners will double by 2000. In LEDCs people are also living longer.

Whether a country is more or less developed, the growing number of old people will be a problem during the 21st century.

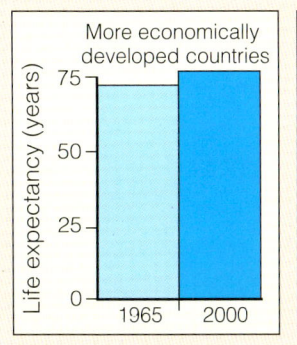

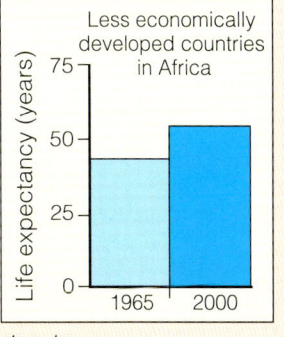

People are living longer

F *Life expectancy increases: people are living longer*

41

3 | People in the countryside

What is life like in the Indian countryside?
Why are there many large families in Indian villages?
What pushes people away from the countryside?

India is an LEDC. Over 900 million people live there and the population is growing. India has been called a nation of villages. Almost seven in every ten of its people live in the 600 000 villages found in the country. Most farm the land. Others work in services or manufacturing for other people in the village. Many villagers are poor in terms of money but have a very rich social life. Life in the village is based around farming, and events like ploughing and harvesting are festival times.

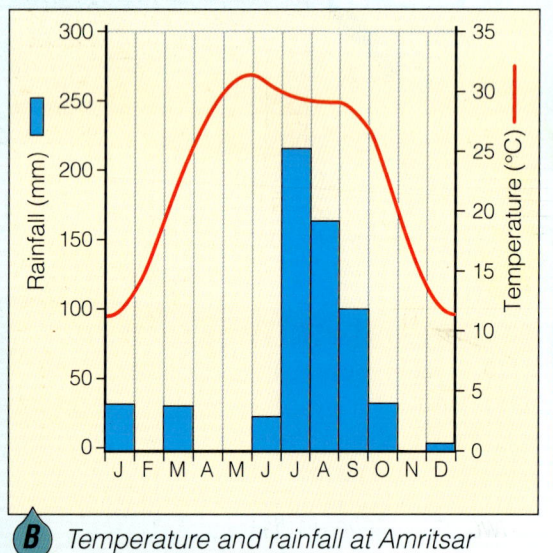

A India

B Temperature and rainfall at Amritsar

C View across water tank to the village

D Advantages of having a large family
- Tend animals
- Collect firewood
- Look after you in old age
- Look after younger children
- Frees adults to earn money

---

1 Look at MAP **A**.
   a What is the direction of Delhi from Amritsar?
   b What is the distance from Amritsar to Delhi?
   c Write a sentence to describe other facts about the location of Amritsar.

2 Look at GRAPH **B**.
   a Complete the following passage:
   At Amritsar most rain falls between the months of _____ and _____.
   For _____ months, between October and _____, very little rain falls.
   b Describe the seasonal pattern of temperature at Amritsar.
   c Suggest a season when the climate may make farming difficult. Explain your choice.

3 Describe the scene in PHOTO **C**.

4 a Use PHOTO **D** to list the advantages of having a large family.
   b Suggest other advantages of your own. Compare these with other members of your class.

42

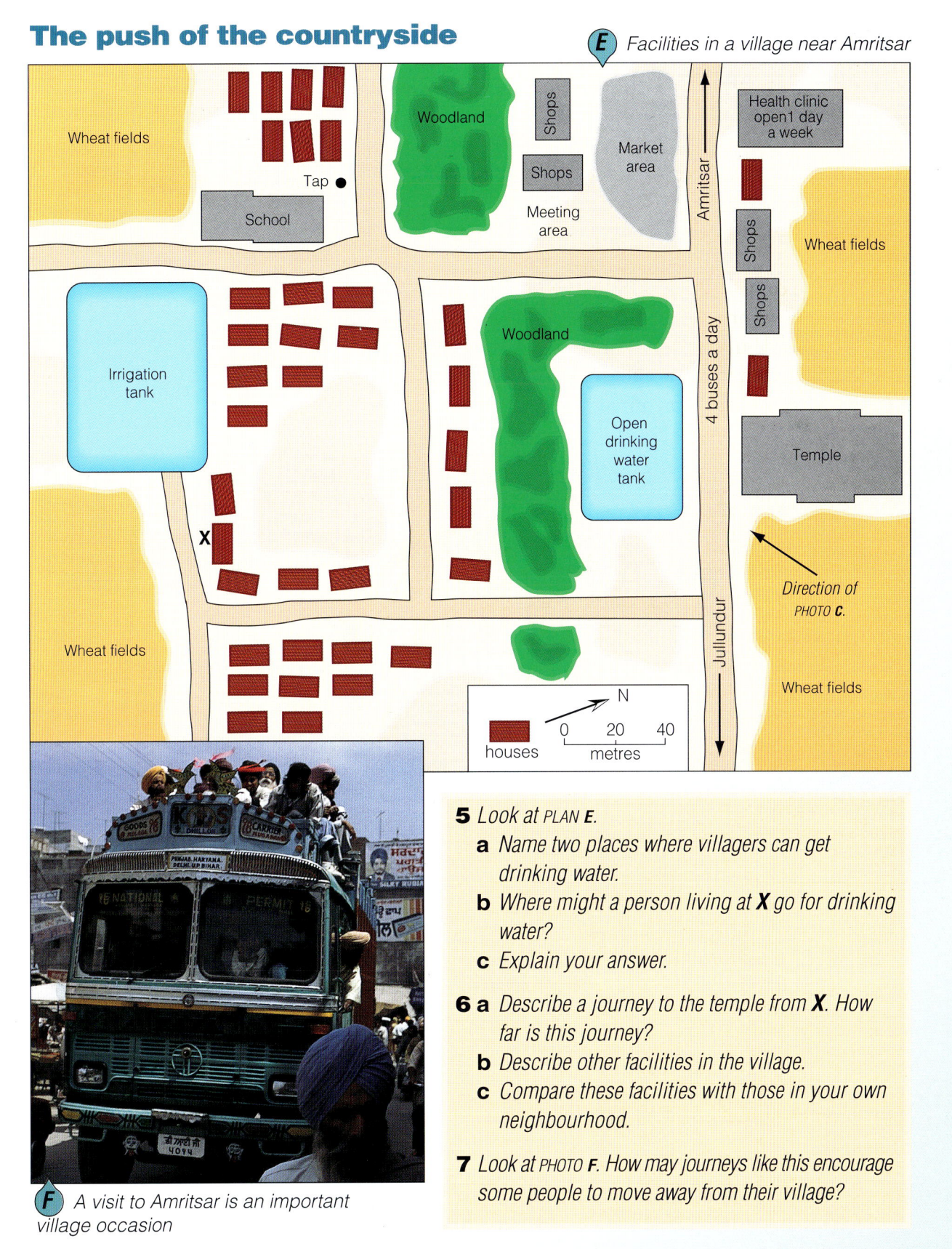

The push of the countryside

E Facilities in a village near Amritsar

F A visit to Amritsar is an important village occasion

5 Look at PLAN **E**.
   a Name two places where villagers can get drinking water.
   b Where might a person living at **X** go for drinking water?
   c Explain your answer.

6 a Describe a journey to the temple from **X**. How far is this journey?
   b Describe other facilities in the village.
   c Compare these facilities with those in your own neighbourhood.

7 Look at PHOTO **F**. How may journeys like this encourage some people to move away from their village?

43

4 | Living in the city

Why are people attracted to cities?
What opportunities for work exist in cities?
Why are families in Indian cities usually smaller than in villages?

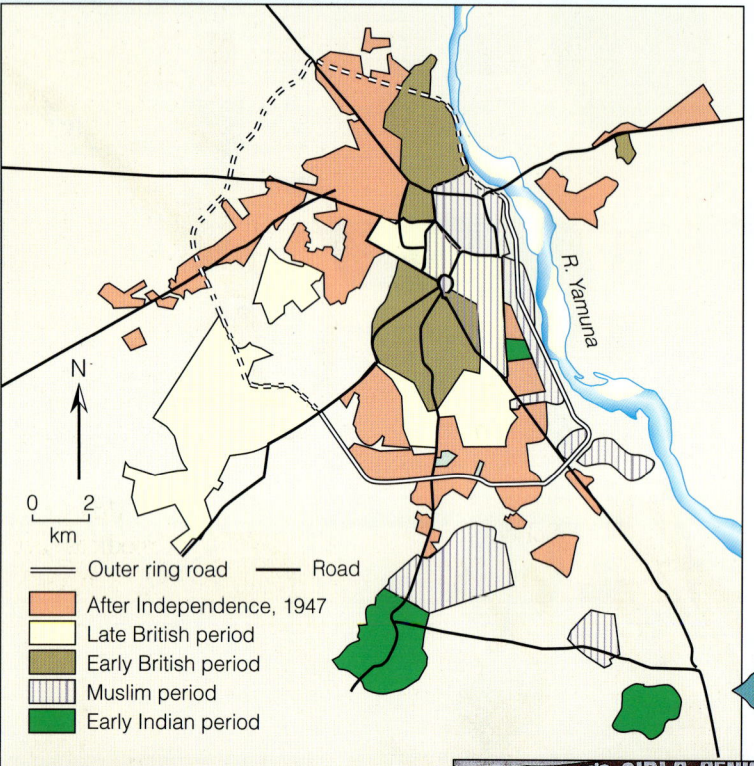

The pull of the city

Many villagers are attracted to cities in India. It is usually the younger people who <u>migrate</u>. This may break up village families, but most <u>migrants</u> have other family or friends to stay with when they reach the city. They will also find some work to do. The movement of large numbers of people into cities, like Delhi, has caused them to expand very quickly. This is called <u>urbanisation</u>.

A Growth of Delhi: since the 1960s growth has been fast and in all directions.

Map legend:
- Outer ring road — Road
- After Independence, 1947
- Late British period
- Early British period
- Muslim period
- Early Indian period

B The city offers many attractions to the villager

---

1 Look at MAP **A**.
  a Describe the location of Delhi in the early Indian period.
  b Describe how Delhi grew after Independence.

2 The hope of better health care is one factor that pulls people from the countryside to the city. Look at PHOTOS **B**.
  a Discuss how the scene in each photo may pull people from the countryside to the city.
  b Make a list of these pull factors.
  c Suggest others and add them to your list.

Getting a job

Many jobs done by migrants are informal. Informal workers are paid in cash for the work they do. They do not pay taxes on their earnings, or work fixed hours. They may, for example clean the houses of richer people. Other jobs are formal. Formal workers are paid a regular wage, pay taxes on their earnings and work fixed hours. Some migrants to Delhi find formal work in factories.

C Working for the local telephone company

D Working for yourself

E Large families in the city could be costly
- School fees
- Private medical care
- Clothes
- Fuel for cooking
- Food must be bought

3 Look at PHOTOS **C** and **D**.
  a Which shows formal work?
  b Suggest other examples of formal work.
  c Which photo shows informal work?
  d Would you prefer formal or informal work? Explain your choice.

4 a Use PHOTO **E** to list the disadvantages of having a large family in the city.
  b Suggest reasons why having a large family in the city is not as useful as one in the countryside.

5 If you lived in an Indian village would you move to a city? Explain your answer.

5 People in Europe

Where are Europe's resources?
Have they influenced where people live?
What is happening to Europe's population?

Europe is the world's smallest <u>continent</u>. It is also the most densely populated. Over 600 million people live here. This is more than 10 per cent of the global population.

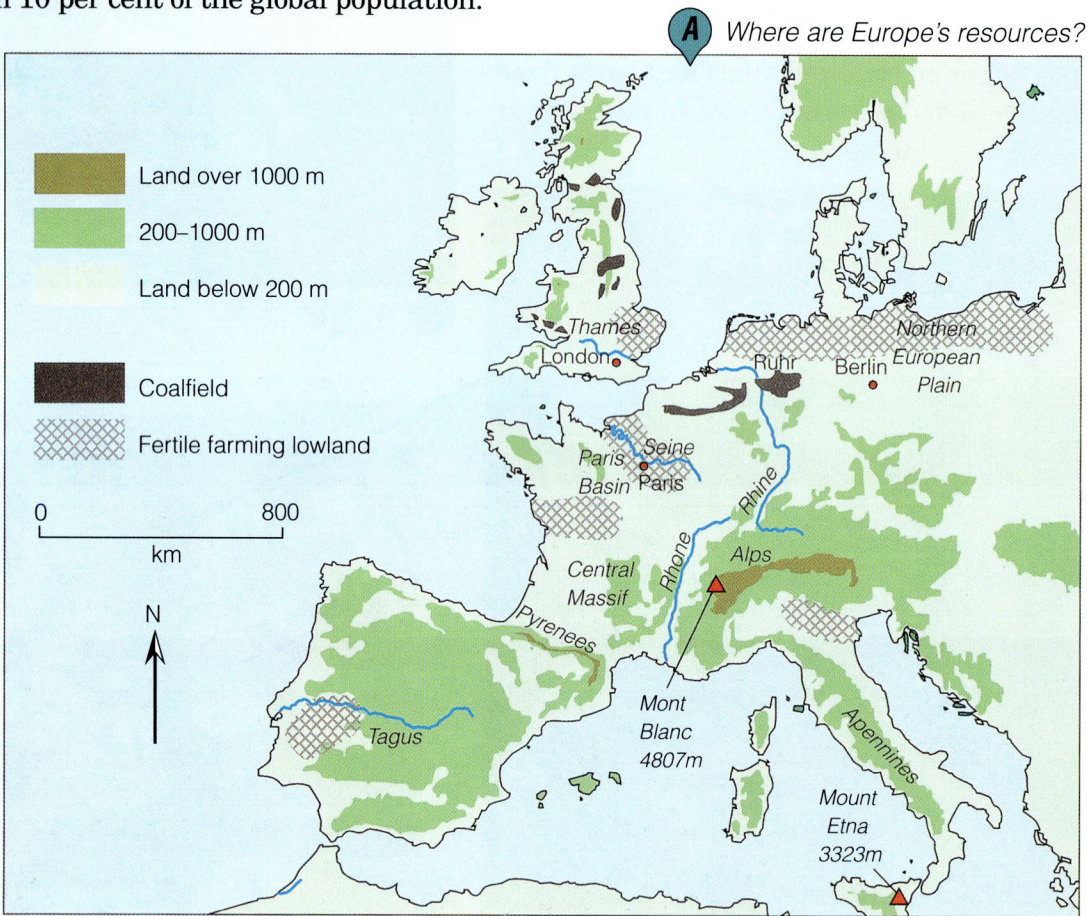

A Where are Europe's resources?

Map legend:
- Land over 1000 m
- 200–1000 m
- Land below 200 m
- Coalfield
- Fertile farming lowland

Scale: 0 – 800 km

Map labels: Thames, London, Ruhr, Berlin, Northern European Plain, Seine, Paris Basin, Paris, Rhine, Rhone, Alps, Central Massif, Pyrenees, Mont Blanc 4807m, Tagus, Apennines, Mount Etna 3323m

---

1 Complete your own outline map of Europe by adding the following from MAP **A**:
  a Mark on the mountain areas over 1000 metres above sea level.
  b Name the • Alps • Apennines • Pyrenees • Central Massif.
  c Locate and name Mont Blanc.
  d Mark on the rivers • Seine • Thames • Rhine • Tagus • Rhone.
  e Shade the Paris Basin.
  f Shade the coalfield areas. Name the Ruhr coalfield.

2 Using evidence from your map:
  a Name two areas where you would not expect to find many people living. Explain your choices.
  b Name three different areas where you think population density might be quite high. Explain why.

People live in different parts of Europe because some sites were easier to live in than others. River valleys provided fertile farmland, shelter and routeways. Rivers provided water and transport. Ports developed on the coasts as trade began between countries.

In the 18th century, coal and iron ore became important new resources for making iron and steel. People left the countryside and moved to work in mines and factories. The factories were built close to where coal was mined. Today, many Europeans still live and work in towns and cities near these coalfields.

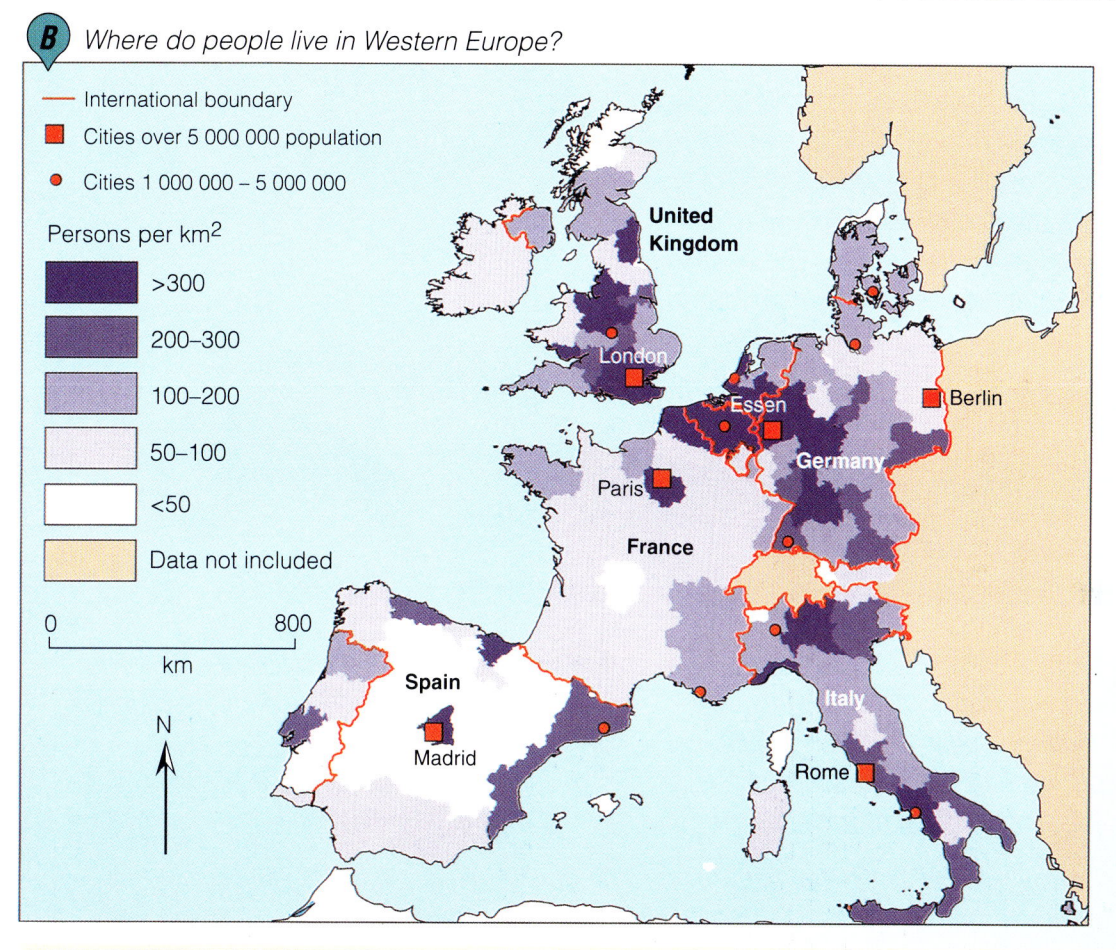

B *Where do people live in Western Europe?*

3 On a tracing overlay of MAP B:
 a Shade areas with more than 300 people per km².
 b Shade areas with less than 50 people per km².
 c How closely do these areas match the height of the land shown on MAP A? Describe any patterns you find.
 d How closely do the areas you have shaded match the answers you gave in Task 2?

4 On your outline, label one area from MAP B which shows:
 - high population density along a river valley
 - low population density over 1000 metres high
 - a coalfield with a high population density
 - a large city with over 5 million people in a fertile farming area

5 Use MAP B to describe the distribution of population in Europe. Mention names of countries and cities.

6 | The Ruhr of Germany

DAS RUHRGEBIET.

How did resources first attract people to the Ruhr region?
Why did people later move away?
What is now being done to attract and keep people?

A The Ruhr industrial region

Moving in for jobs

Before 1750, iron was made in small amounts in forest locations. People burnt charcoal to heat iron ore.

After 1750, the Industrial Revolution began in Europe. People then burnt coal to change iron into steel. This is a much stronger metal. Many people migrated to work in coal mines and factories, which grew up on the coalfields. The biggest coalfield in Europe is the Ruhr in Germany.

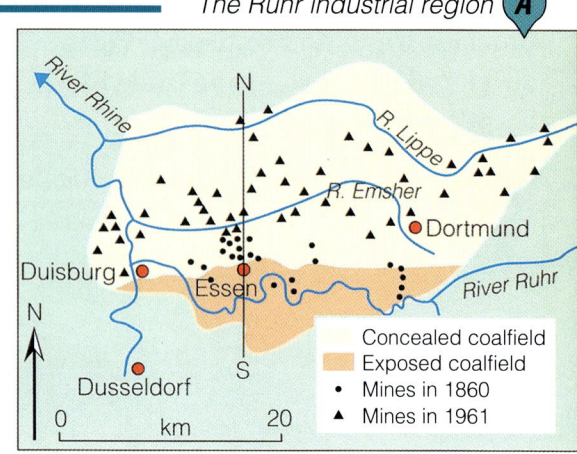

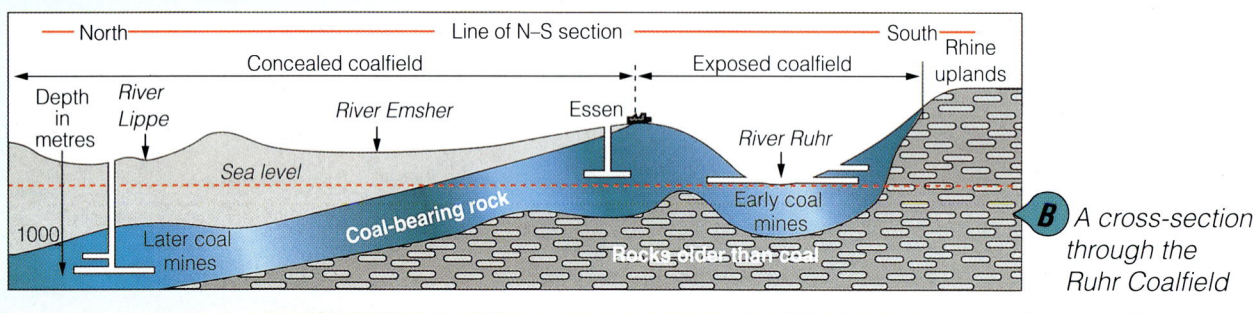

B A cross-section through the Ruhr Coalfield

---

1 Study MAP A on page 46.
  a Describe the location of the Ruhr region in relation to: • London • Paris • Berlin.
  b Why do you think the Ruhr was known as 'the industrial heartland of Europe'?

2 a On a copy of the map of the Ruhr industrial region (MAP A) add:
  • the exposed and concealed coalfields
  • the four rivers
  • the towns of Essen, Duisburg, and Dortmund.
  • the mines in 1860.
  b What do you understand by an exposed coalfield?
  c How is a concealed coalfield different?

3 a Use evidence from MAP A and SECTION B to explain why many 19th century migrants to the Ruhr lived in Essen.

4 a Add to your map the location of 1961 mines.
  b Explain why the location of mines changed between 1860 and 1961.
  c Suggest how this may have affected patterns of migration in the coalfield area.

5 Study GRAPH C. Copy and complete the following paragraph.
In 1895 there were nearly _____ people living in the Ruhr region. This figure rose rapidly to over 4 million in 1939 when the _____ World War began. People then left to join the services, and coal and steel production fell. The most rapid population increase was in the 15 years from 1946 to 19__ . In this period there was an increase of 1.6 million from 3.9 million to _____.
After 1961 people began to move away and the population fell. But since _____ there has been a slight increase to 5.4 million.

48

C *Population change in the Ruhr region, 1895–1995*

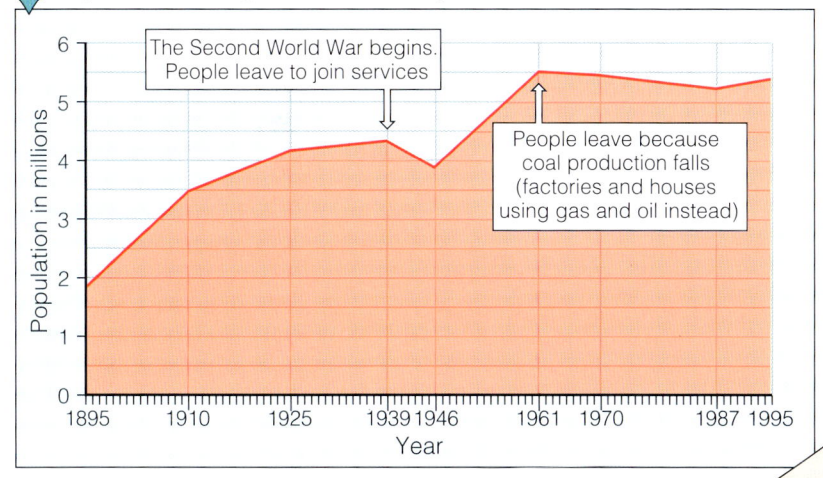

The Second World War begins. People leave to join services

People leave because coal production falls (factories and houses using gas and oil instead)

New faces in coal places: minister for the Ruhr region

D Since 1961 the demand for coal has fallen. This is because power stations and homes began using gas and oil. Jobs were lost so people left the Ruhr. Since then, we have spent money to improve the Ruhr. There are new universities, like Essen. Hi-Technology centres are retraining people with new skills. We have cleaned the environment and we have new arts and leisure industries.

Today over 5.4 million people live here. Many who left are coming back. They are surprised by the new Ruhr.

E *Smoke from factory furnaces, Essen, 1895*

F *An improved environment in Essen, 1997*

6 Study SPEECH **D**.
  a Why did the Ruhr industries decline after 1961?
  b Suggest why people moved away from the Ruhr.
  c What did the German government do to try and keep people in the Ruhr?

7 Compare PHOTOS **E** and **F**.
  a List how Essen's environment has changed.
  b You are trying to attract new business and people to the Ruhr region. Design a publicity leaflet using Essen as an example of how the Ruhr has changed.

7 People in French villages

**Why are some farming communities in decline?
How are village functions changing?**

A The location of Limousin

B Farming is the traditional work in Limousin

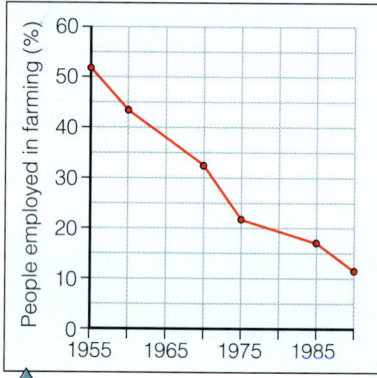

Unlike the Ruhr industrial area, the Limousin area of France relies on farming. The soil is poor, though, and the area gets about 1400 mm of rain a year. (London has only 593 mm of rain a year.) Limousin winters are cold, and snow falls for up to fifty days a year. Some land is used for grazing and for growing hay to feed cattle and sheep. In the summer, many tourists visit.

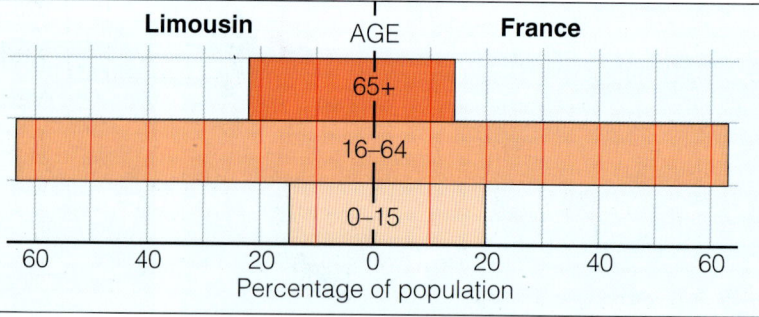

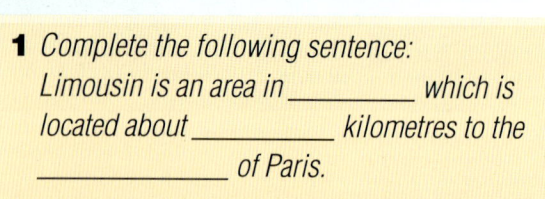

C Limousin is changing

D Population pyramid

1 Complete the following sentence:
Limousin is an area in _____ which is located about _____ kilometres to the _____ of Paris.

2 a Label a sketch of PHOTO **B** to show facts about Limousin's soils, farming and vegetation.
  b Add short sentences to describe the climate.

3 a What does GRAPH **C** tell you about changes in employment in farming?
  b Use DIAGRAM **E** to explain why these changes have taken place.

4 Look at GRAPH **D**.
  a Describe the main differences between the population of Limousin and the rest of France.
  b Suggest what is likely to happen to Limousin's population in future. Explain your answer.

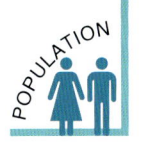

Changing villages

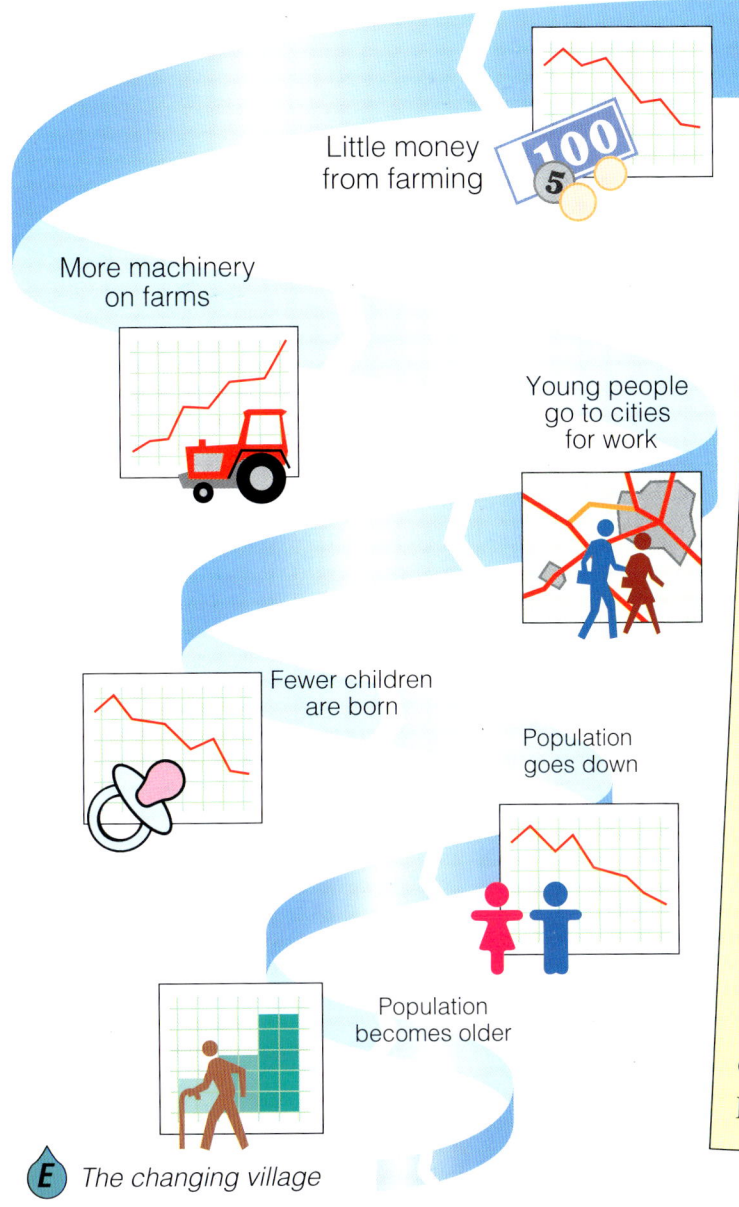

Little money from farming

More machinery on farms

Young people go to cities for work

Fewer children are born

Population goes down

Population becomes older

E The changing village

Advertisement for an old farm turned into a holiday home **F**

FLAYAT
Coulignat   **2/3 bedrooms: capacity 6**
Location: Scenic rural setting, 80 km south-east of Gueret. Easy access both to the scenic Auvergne with its many lakes and rivers, and to the beautiful upper valley of the Dordogne.
Shopping 5 km. Lake for sailing, canoeing swimming and fishing. Horse-riding.

French Life Holidays

As the population decreases, many buildings become unused. Some are bought by people from French cities to use as weekend or retirement homes. Others are advertised in holiday brochures in the UK.

5 a *Describe what is happening in* DIAGRAM **E**.
  b *How may this affect village services?*
  c *Suggest a suitable title for the spiral.*

6 *Look at* ADVERT **F**.
  a *Describe the location of the house.*
  b *Make a list of the natural features which attract people to this area.*

7 *Suggest how the use of many houses as holiday homes may affect people who live in the area. Mention both good and bad effects.*

51

8 Change in the UK

When was the UK like an LEDC?
How were birth and death rates reduced?
What is happening to the UK's population today?

The United Kingdom was once much less economically developed than it is now.

Most people lived in small settlements spread around the countryside. There were a few towns, where people bought and sold produce at weekly markets. Larger towns included London, and other ports like Bristol and Liverpool.

Development in the UK was the result of several factors. These included a better diet, better housing and more education. People's health improved. At the same time, birth rates and death rates started to fall.

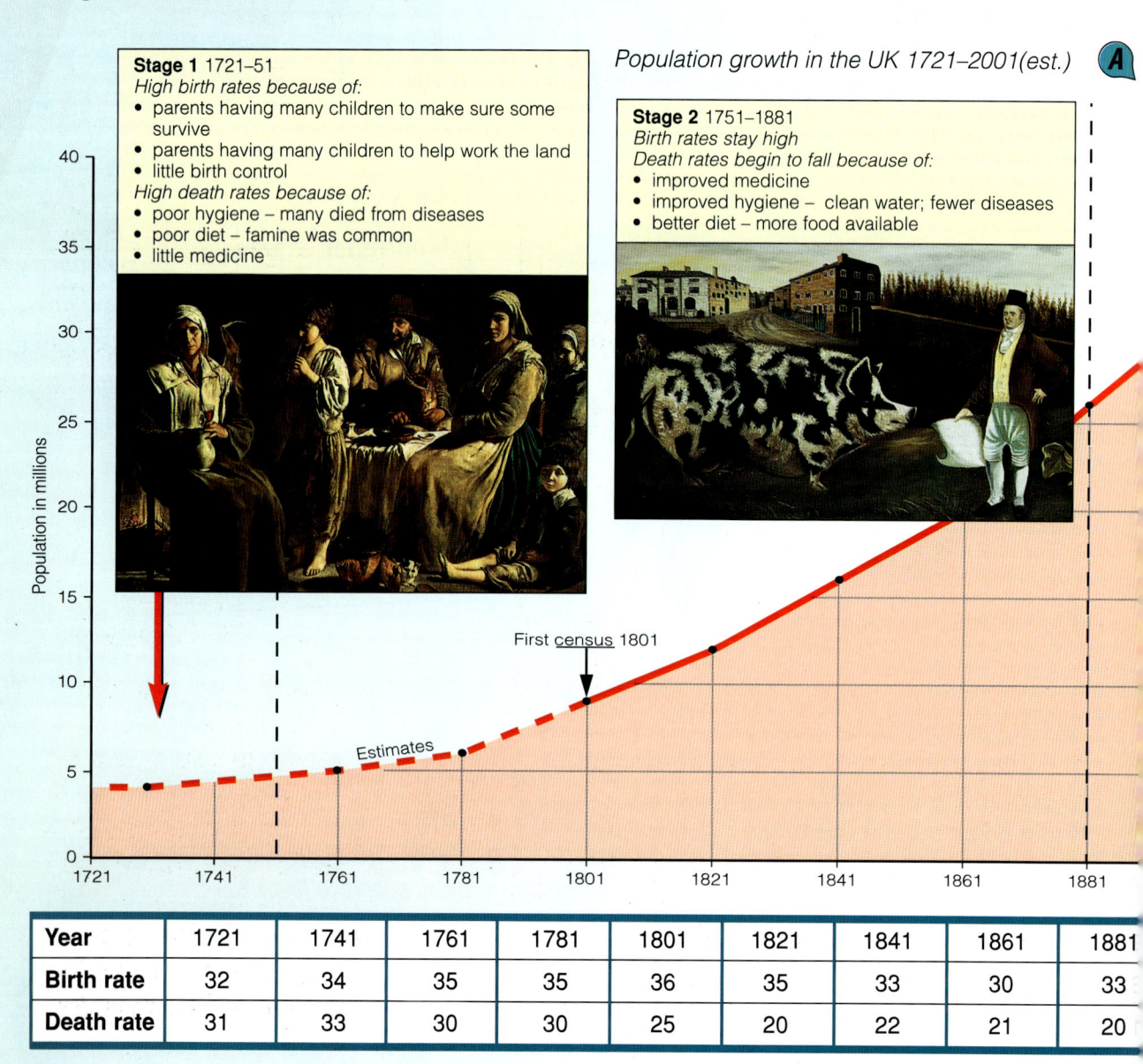

Stage 1 1721–51
High birth rates because of:
- parents having many children to make sure some survive
- parents having many children to help work the land
- little birth control

High death rates because of:
- poor hygiene – many died from diseases
- poor diet – famine was common
- little medicine

Population growth in the UK 1721–2001(est.) **A**

Stage 2 1751–1881
Birth rates stay high
Death rates begin to fall because of:
- improved medicine
- improved hygiene – clean water; fewer diseases
- better diet – more food available

First census 1801

Estimates

Year	1721	1741	1761	1781	1801	1821	1841	1861	1881
Birth rate	32	34	35	35	36	35	33	30	33
Death rate	31	33	30	30	25	20	22	21	20

52

8 POPULATION

Stage 3 1881–1931
Birth rates fall because of:
- family planning
- industry and employment which reduces the need for so many children

Death rates continue to fall because of:
- better hospitals and medicine

Stage 4 1931–present
Low birth rates because:
- people are choosing to have fewer babies

Low death rates because:
- there is more care for the elderly
- more medical improvements

BIRTH RATE = NUMBER OF BABIES BORN IN A YEAR FOR EACH 1000 PEOPLE
DEATH RATE = NUMBER OF PEOPLE WHO DIE IN A YEAR FOR EACH 1000 PEOPLE
BOTH RATES RANGE FROM LESS THAN 15 (LOW) TO OVER 30 (HIGH).

1 Study GRAPH **A**. Complete these sentences:
- The birth rate tells you how many…
- Over 30 births per 1000 people is…
- The death rate tells you how many…
- Fewer than 15 deaths per 1000 people per year is ….

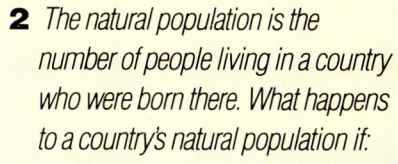

2 The natural population is the number of people living in a country who were born there. What happens to a country's natural population if:
   a birth rates are higher than death rates?
   b death rates are higher than birth rates?

3 The UK has four stages in its development. Use GRAPH **A** to copy and complete the table below to identify each stage.

Stage	Dates	Death rate	Birth rate
1	1721–51	High	High

4 a From TABLE **B** list the UK's birth and death rates in • 1751 and • 1981.
   b Compare the rates in 1751 with 1981.
   c Write a few sentences to describe life in the UK:
   - when it was an LEDC (before 1751)
   - as an MEDC (since 1931).

5 a What was the population of the UK in 1801?
   b How can we know this is an accurate figure?
   c Describe the trend in total UK population between 1801 and 1991.
   d How is the UK population likely to change after 2000?
   e Suggest some reasons for this.

	1921	1941	1961	1981	2001
30	22	15	17	13	?
7	15	12	10	12	?

B UK birth and death rates

53

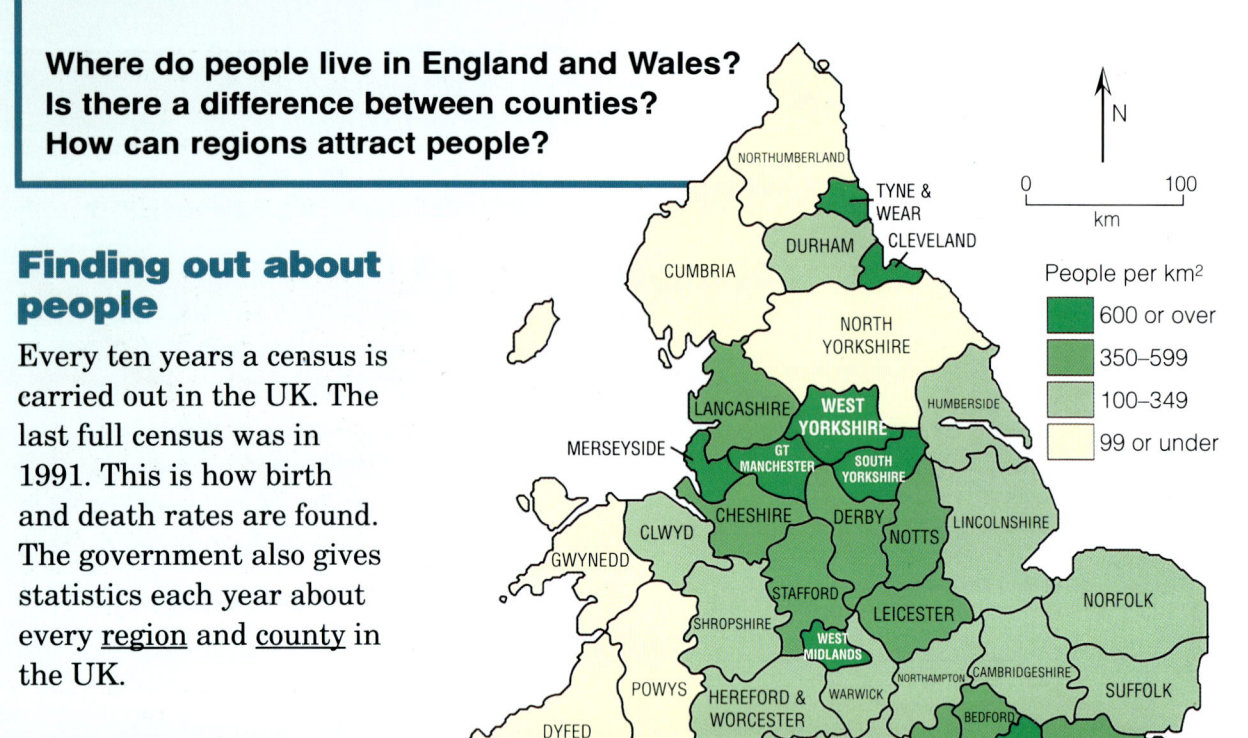

9 | Differences in the UK

Where do people live in England and Wales?
Is there a difference between counties?
How can regions attract people?

Finding out about people

Every ten years a census is carried out in the UK. The last full census was in 1991. This is how birth and death rates are found. The government also gives statistics each year about every <u>region</u> and <u>county</u> in the UK.

Population density for counties in England and Wales, 1991 **A**

People per km²
- 600 or over
- 350–599
- 100–349
- 99 or under

---

1 a How often does the census take place?
  b Suggest why the government gives statistics between each census.

2 Find your own county on MAP A. Compare its population density with other counties in your region.

3 Look at MAP A and the map of regions on page 35.
  a Work out which counties match the statements below.
  - A county close to Scotland with 100–349 people per km².
  - A long, narrow county in Wales with 99 or fewer people per km².
  - The most densely populated county in the Midlands region.
  - Two densely populated counties in the far North of England.
  b Describe the distribution of counties in England and Wales with 99 or fewer people per square km².
  c Use relief and climate maps of the UK to explain why so few people live in these areas.
  d Which counties in England and Wales are the most crowded?
  e Use an atlas to help explain this pattern.

Comparing two counties

Cumbria is a county with only 72 people per km².

The mountains of the Lake District are used for sheep farming and attract hillwalkers. The lakes also bring in tourists and provide income all year, but especially in the summer.

Carlisle is the largest town in Cumbria, with 104 000 people.

B *Cumbria: a county in the North-West of England*

Surrey is a county with 623 people per km². It is in the South-East region. This is one of the fastest growing regions in the UK. Many people commute to London to work in offices.

Guildford is the largest town in Surrey with 125 000 people.

C *Surrey: a county in the South-East of England*

	Cumbria	Surrey
Total population	490 000	1 044 000
Population growth rate 1981–95	2%	3%
Birth rate	11	12
Death rate	12	10
Unemployment	5%	2%

D *Two counties compared (1995 data)*   Regional Trends 1997

4 Use MAP **A** and EXTRACTS **B** and **C** to complete two factfiles for • Cumbria and • Surrey. Include facts on the following:
- location
- size of county
- population density
- jobs.

5 Study TABLE **D**.
  a Which county has: • the lower birth rate • the higher death rate • the lower population growth rate?
  b Suggest how Cumbria's population could grow even if birth rates remain less than death rates.
  c Cumbria is trying to create more jobs. Use TABLE **D** to explain why.

6 Study ADVERT **E**.
  a Which three reasons would most attract a new business to Cumbria? Explain why.
  b Design an advert to attract people to live and work in your county or city.

CARLISLE
The Great Border City

Carlisle is one of the most successful cities in Britain. Home to over 100 000 people, it offers excellent business opportunities and a good quality of life.

✓ Regular air services to London and Liverpool from Carlisle airport
✓ Links to major cities by West Coast inter-city rail
✓ M6 and A69 link to national road networks
✓ Wide range of courses at Carlisle University
✓ Cheap land available in many areas
✓ A market of 3 million tourists and 0.5 million residents
✓ Grants and loans available from the EU
✓ An attractive area for working

E *Come and join us!*

10 Moving to another country

Why do people migrate?
How do migrants help the countries to which they move?

People migrate from one country to another for different reasons. Some move to find better jobs. Others want to be closer to family members. These pull factors attract migrants to their new countries.

Other people are forced out of the country where they were born by push factors. These migrants could be escaping poverty, war or a natural disaster, like a flood.

> Indians can now get work permits from the British government. It is expected that many will go to the UK. They will look for work in clothing and footwear firms, food and drink plants, car manufacturing, the elecrical industry and in transport.

A UK welcomes immigrant workers in the 1950s

I read in the newspaper in 1958 that England needed extra workers. At the time I was working in Delhi as a civil servant.

Leaving family and friends to go to Nottingham was a difficult decision to make.

We were expected to dress in a way which is strange to our culture.

I worked hard and got a more responsible job.

We spent much of the money we earned on starting our own business.

Now we are retired. My children all have good jobs and also help to run our business.

B Storyboard: a migrant from Delhi comes to work on the buses in Nottingham

---

1 Look at ARTICLE **A**.
  a What jobs were available?
  b Discuss why there were vacancies for these jobs in the UK.

2 Look at STORYBOARD **B**.
  a Suggest why Mr Sandhu decided to move to Nottingham.
  b Explain why it was a difficult decision.
  c List two important decisions made by the family after arriving in Nottingham. Explain your choice.
  d Why might Mr Sandhu feel that he made the right decision in 1958?

56

10

POPULATION

C Helping to keep Britain healthy

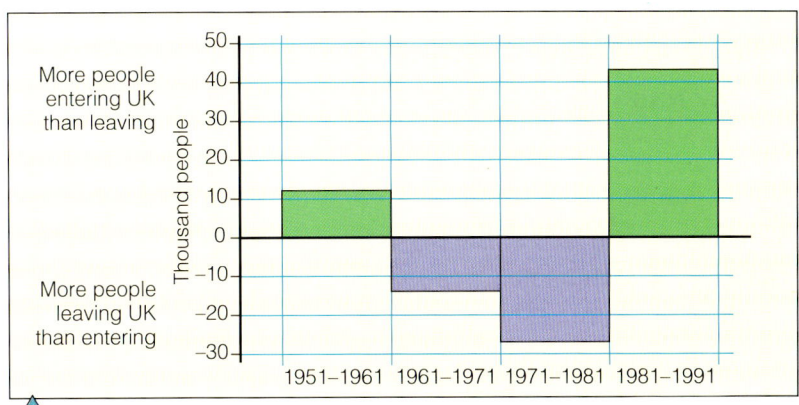

D United Kingdom: Migration 1951–91

The New Commonwealth is a group of countries that recognise the British Queen as their Head of State.

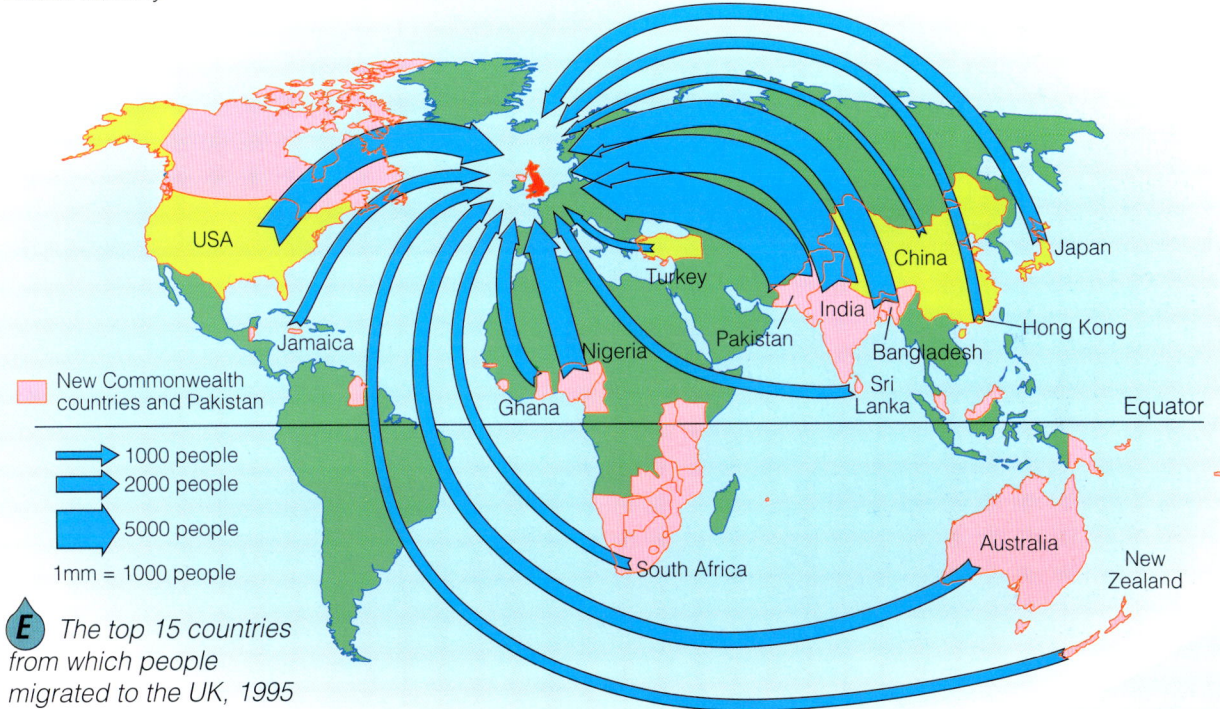

E The top 15 countries from which people migrated to the UK, 1995

3 Using PHOTO **C** and other information from these pages explain how migrants and their families helped development in the UK.

4 Look at GRAPH **D**.
  a Describe what happened to migration between 1951 and 1981.
  b How did this change after 1981?

5 Look at MAP **E**.
  a List the five countries from which most people migrated to the UK in 1995.
  b What do these countries all have in common?
  c Suggest why people from these countries migrated to the UK.

6 Put yourself in the position of either Mr Sandhu or the nurse after 30 years in the UK. Write a letter home to describe your feelings about your move and the way things have worked out.

57

11 | A rich society

How have migrants adapted to British life?
How has migration enriched British society?

When people from abroad arrive in a new city, it is natural for them to decide to live near their relatives or other immigrants who have come from the same country. They will then be close to others who speak the same language. Shops change and places of worship grow to meet the needs of migrants. In this way, they keep their traditional cultures, and also learn about their new country. The new cultures they bring enrich the lives of the people who have always lived there.

A New eating experiences

B Sikh temple

C Rich colours in traditional clothing

11

As the children and grandchildren of migrants become successful, some move away from the areas which their parents <u>settled</u>. They have moved outwards from the <u>inner city</u> towards the <u>suburbs</u>. For these people, places of worship, specialist shops and entertainment centres are even more important than for those people who prefer to stay.

D *Supporting the community*

E *Sketch map of part of West Nottingham (not to scale)*

Key

Origins
- Bangladesh/Pakistan
- India
- West Indies
- Hong Kong
- Europe

Function
- R Place of worship
- D Restaurant/take-away
- E Culture/entertainment
- G Grocer's shop
- C Clothes shop

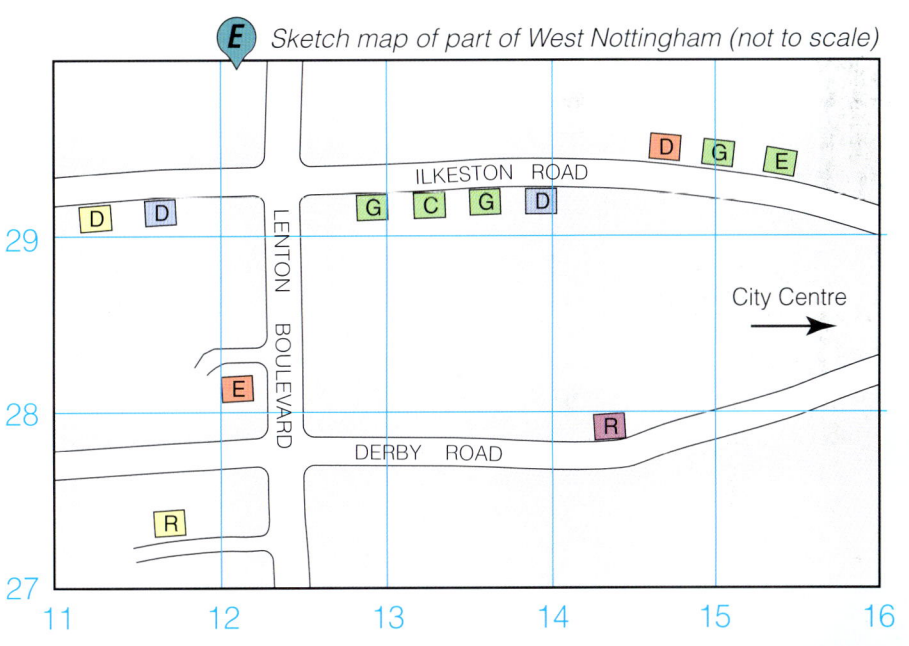

---

1 PHOTOS **A** to **D** are places found on MAP **E**.
   a Give the grid references of the squares in which each photo was taken.
   b Describe how the scenes in each photo help to enrich the lives of people living in the city.

2 Look at MAP **E**.
   a A Greek Orthodox church is shown on the map. What is its grid reference?
   b Complete a copy of the table on the right by adding each feature shown on the map. The first one has been done for you.

Feature	Location	Origin
Restaurant Take-away food	1129	Hong Kong

3 a Discuss why some people wish to move away from the inner city and others wish to stay.
   b Why might the facilities on MAP **E** be even more important to those who have moved to the suburbs?

4 Would you wish to move away from your home area? Explain your decision.

59

12 The global village

What pushes people away from cities?
What barriers are there against travelling to work?
How may technology affect future settlement patterns?

More than ever before people living in cities suffer from asthma because of pollution from traffic **A**

Many people in MEDCs feel tired of city life. They say that as cities have grown, living in them has become more difficult and unpleasant. Some people have bought houses in villages near to the cities where they work. They travel by car or train each day to their place of work. These people are called <u>commuters</u>.

C Large numbers of people travel by train during the morning and evening rush hours

B City crime rates are rising

D Commuting to work by car does not always mean arriving on time

1 a Describe the scene in PHOTO **A**.
 b Explain how it may affect the lives of people living in these houses.

2 a What is SIGN **B** suggesting people should do?
 b Why is it suggesting this?

3 a Discuss other disadvantages of living in a city.
 b Explain why many people now live in the countryside.

4 a What is a commuter?
 b What impression of commuting to you get from PHOTOS **C** and **D**?
 c Would you prefer to live near, or away from, your place of work? Explain your decision.

60

The old market town of Villena has recently become a town of the future. Almost half of its 30000 people have direct access to a computer. The figure is growing rapidly. Houses and businesses were given the chance of buying them at half price. The computers are linked to a 'Virtual Town Hall' and it is possible to do much of the day's work without leaving home. There are plans to extend beyond Villena to link up the four million inhabitants in the surrounding region. Seven towns in the UK, Germany, Italy and Denmark are about to take part in similar projects funded by the European Union.

E *No more commuting to work!*

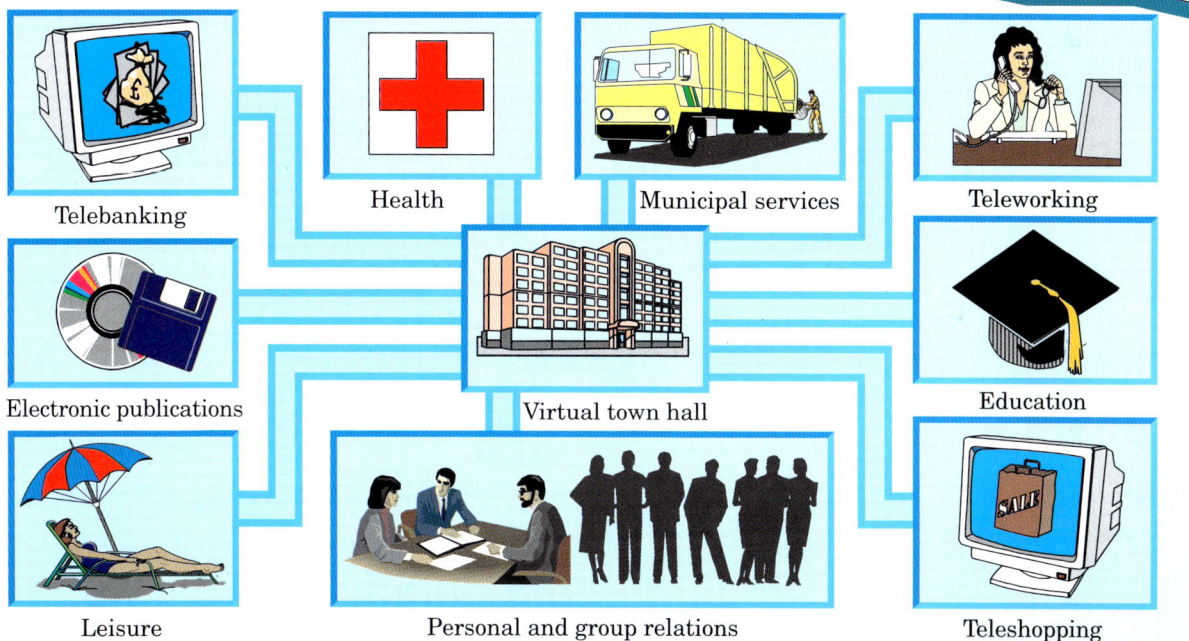

- Telebanking
- Health
- Municipal services
- Teleworking
- Electronic publications
- Virtual town hall
- Education
- Leisure
- Personal and group relations
- Teleshopping

F *Linking with the 'Virtual Town Hall'*

The European, 29 May–4 June 1997

5 Use ARTICLE **E**.
  a Describe the location of Villena.
  b Suggest why it is thought of as a town of the future.

6 Look at DIAGRAM **F**.
  a Describe the importance of the 'Virtual Town Hall'.
  b Suggest which feature you would use to:
    • make a doctor's appointment
    • learn about Geography • pay the rent on your house • order a pizza.
  c Explain how this system helps people to work from home.
  d Discuss which groups of workers • may and • may not be able to work from home.

7 To what extent might new technology affect where people live and work?

Population glossary

Census
A count of all the people in a country. It usually includes information about their houses and the jobs they do. In the UK, the census takes place every 10 years e.g. 1981, 1991, 2001.

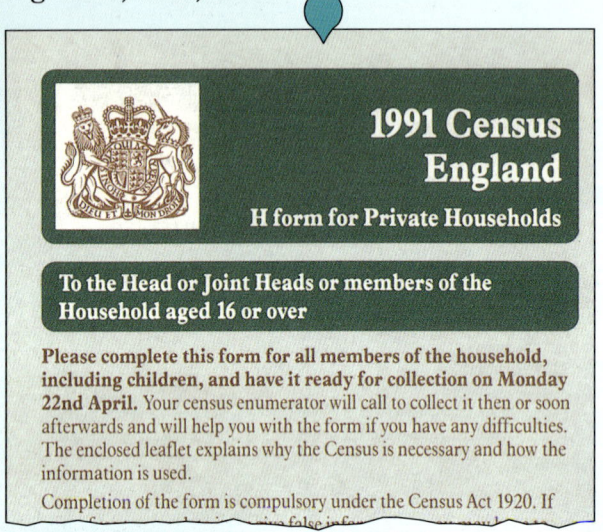

Commute
To travel each day to and from work, usually by car or train.

Commuter
A person who **commutes** to and from work.

Continent
A very large area of land.

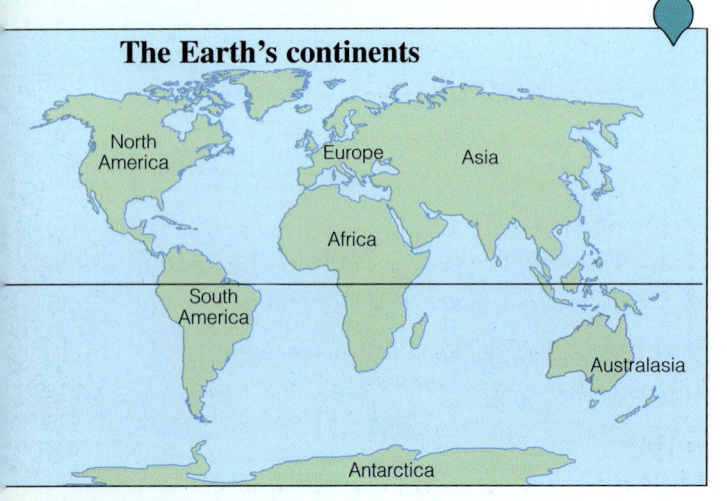

The Earth's continents

County
The UK is divided into smaller areas called counties e.g. Northamptonshire. Each county is run by its own local council.

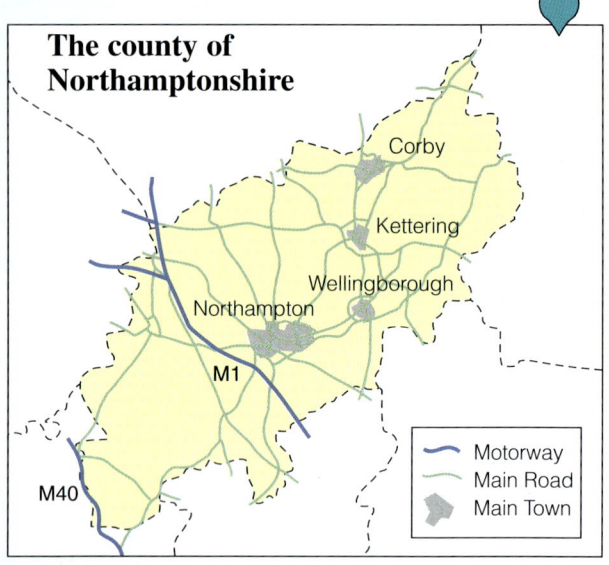

The county of Northamptonshire

Distribution
A pattern that tells you where more than one place or activity is located e.g. where several shops are located in a city.

Festival
An organized event or celebration e.g. Easter, Divali.

Formal work
Work that takes place during fixed hours and pays a regular wage e.g. working in a factory.

High population density
When a large number of people live in a certain area. Population density is usually measured in people per km².

Immigrant
A person who moves permanently to live in a new place. This is usually another country.

Industrial Revolution
A period in a country's development when large numbers of people leave farming to work in factories in cities.

Informal work
Work which has no set hours and no regular wages. e.g. shoe-shining, window cleaning.

Inner city
The area surrounding the Central Business District (CBD). Here, many old houses and factories may have been replaced, or are being replaced. The inner city is closer to the CBD than the **suburbs**.

Low population density
When few people live in a particular area. Population density is usually measured in people per km^2.

Manufacturing
Making products by hand, or by using machinery. This usually occurs in a factory.

Migrant
A person who **migrates**.

Migrate
To move from one place to **settle** in another.

Nation
A single country. Each nation has its own capital city where the national government is based.

Pull factors
Reasons why people are attracted to settle in another area/country, such as better jobs, better education.

Push factors
Reasons why people are forced to move away from an area to settle in another area/country, such as drought in rural areas, war.

Region
An area within a country which has definite boundaries for a function or purpose. For example, East Anglia is a region in the east of England.

Resources
Materials or skills that people find useful. For example, coal is a natural resource which people use for fuel.

Service
An economic activity that provides for people's needs. Many people work in a service e.g. hairdressing, transport, business.

Settle
To move into an area to live there permanently.

Site
The land on which a place is built. For example where a village is built, or a factory.

Suburb
The outer part of a town or city. Inner and outer suburbs are always outside the inner city and the Central Business District (CBD).

Urbanisation
When the number of people living in towns and cities increases. This may be because many people **migrate** from the countryside into cities looking for work.

Valley
A low area between hills which usually contains a river.

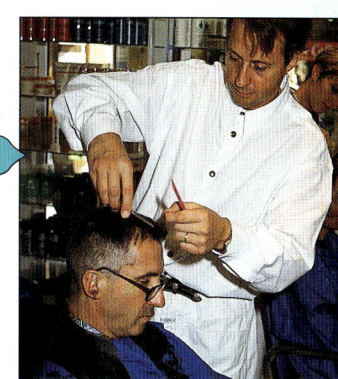

The next step is yours ...

Israel in the sea

Israel plans to dump earth into the sea and create 40 offshore islands. Each will have flats built on it for 20 000 people. This will help solve the problem of a growing population in a small country. Israel's population is expected to rise to over 6 million in 2003, an increase of 1 million people since 1991. Each new small town will be linked to the mainland by bridges.

Major new building developments on the Israeli coast at Eilat

After: The Sunday Times, 9 Feb, 1997

City	Population (million)
Tokyo	28.7
Mumbai (Bombay)	27.4
Lagos	24.4
Shanghai	23.4
Jakarta	21.2
Sao Paulo	20.8
Karachi	20.6
Peking	19.4
Dhaka	19.0
Mexico City	18.8

A *The ten largest cities in 2015?*

B *Making more space*

The population is increasing in most regions of the world. Birth rates remain high in many countries. Everywhere, people are living longer. Better medical facilities and improved diets are causing a world population explosion. If basic needs are to be met for all these people there must be more space or better use of existing space.

Some scientists think that in future, wars will be caused by people needing more space, food, water and housing. How can this be prevented?

1 *Look at TABLE A.*
  a *Copy the table and add a third column with the heading 'Country'.*
  b *Use an atlas to name the country in which each of the ten growing cities is located.*
  c *How many of these cities are in MEDCs, and how many are in LEDCs?*

2 *Read ARTICLE B.*
  a *What problem is Israel planning to solve?*
  b *How is it planning to solve its problem?*
  c *Do you think this is a good idea? Give your reasons.*

3 a *Discuss other ways that countries could solve the problems of having so many people.*
  b *Prepare a two-minute talk on your ideas. Present it to the class.*

Earthquakes & Volcanoes

Mount Ruapehu erupts on North Island, New Zealand 17 June 1996

The Hanshin Expressway in Kobe, Japan, after an earthquake 17 January 1995

**Imagine taking these photos.
What would you have seen, heard and felt?**

1 Natural hazards

What are earthquakes like?
What are volcanoes like?
Where do they happen?
What damage can they cause?

Exciting times!

What words remind you of earthquakes?

What words remind you of volcanoes?

> fire, loud, quiet, wind, dramatic, ice, noisy, earth, sea, smoke, ash, shaking, dust, moving, rumbling, thrilling, damage, deaths, dull, dangerous.

A Earthquakes and volcanoes wordbox

B A rescue team searches for survivors after an earthquake in Maharashtra, India (October 1993)

C A victim of the Mount Pinatubo eruption is carried through streets covered with thick ash, the Philippines (June 1991)

D Fires from a broken gas pipe burn down houses, while water floods the street after an earthquake, Los Angeles, USA (January 1994)

1 Look at WORDBOX **A**.
  a Make two lists of words; one for earthquakes and one for volcanoes. Choose some from the wordbox then add some of your own.

2 Compare your lists with others in your class.

1 EARTHQUAKES & VOLCANOES

Iceland faces flooding as volcano melts vast glacier
6 November 1996

14 November 1996
Miners trapped underground by earthquake in southern Peru

Chinese earthquake causes landslide deaths near Peking
20 November 1996

E Earthquakes and volcanoes: November news!

Month/year	Country	Earthquake location
October 1993	India	Maharashtra

F Earthquakes: when did they happen?

Month/year	Country	Volcanic eruption
June 1991	The Philippine Islands	Mount Pinatubo

G Volcanic eruptions: when did they happen?

3 Use page 65, PHOTOS **B**, **C**, **D** and an atlas to help with this task.
  a On a world map, mark the location of these five places:
  Kobe, Japan
  North Island, New Zealand
  The Philippine Islands
  Los Angeles, USA
  Maharashtra, India.
  b Mark on your map whether an earthquake (E) or volcano (V) took place there. (You could invent symbols of your own.)
  c Use PHOTOS **B**, **C** and **D** to label how people were affected by the events.

4 Read the headlines in **E**. They are taken from newspapers for just one month.
  a Add to your world map the location of the places in **E**.
  b Label your map to show the effects of these earthquakes and volcanoes on people.

5 Make a copy of TABLES **F** and **G**. Use the information on these pages to list the earthquakes and volcanoes in time order.

2 | Living dangerously

Where do earthquakes take place?
Where do volcanoes erupt?
Which cities and countries are living dangerously?

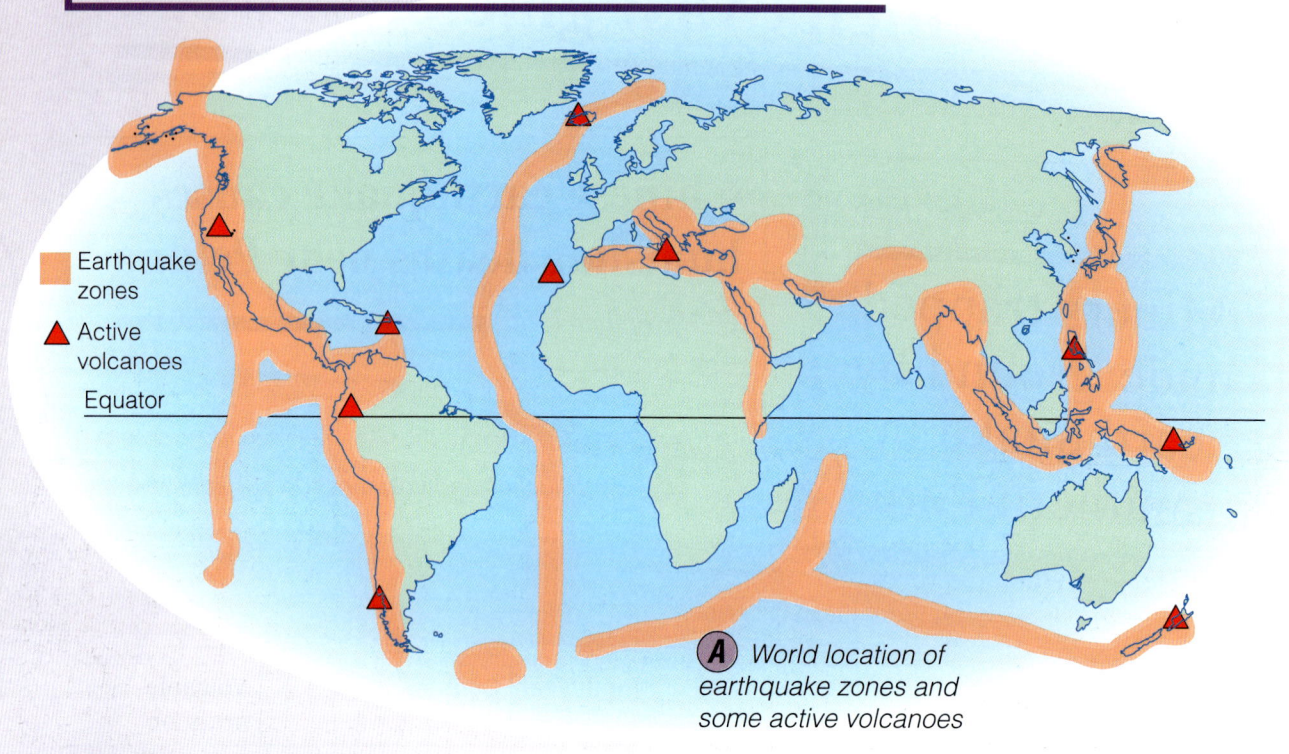

A World location of earthquake zones and some active volcanoes

Where on earth...?

Some people think that earthquakes and volcanic eruptions can happen anywhere. Is it just a matter of luck? The zones on MAP A show where the most recent earthquakes and eruptions took place.

The British Geological Survey is based in Edinburgh. It records all earthquakes happening in the world. There are more than you may think. We only hear about the ones that do most damage. In 1995, over 750 important earthquakes were recorded.

Mount St Helens, Washington, USA	Mount Pinatubo, Philippines
Montserrat Island, West Indies	Raboul, Papua New Guinea
Nevado del Ruiz, Colombia	Ruapehu, New Zealand
La Palma, Canary Islands	El Llaima, Chile
Mount Etna, Sicily	Loki, Iceland

B Ten active volcanoes: where **not** to go for your holidays!

1 Look at MAP A and use an atlas.
   a Copy the earthquake zones from MAP A on your world map.
   b Where is the earthquake zone in North America?
   c Describe the location of two other areas where earthquakes take place.

2 Name two areas of the world that are not in earthquakes zones.

3 The active volcanoes in TABLE B are located on MAP A.
   a Add and name these active volcanoes on your own world map.
   b How closely do the volcano locations match earthquake zones?

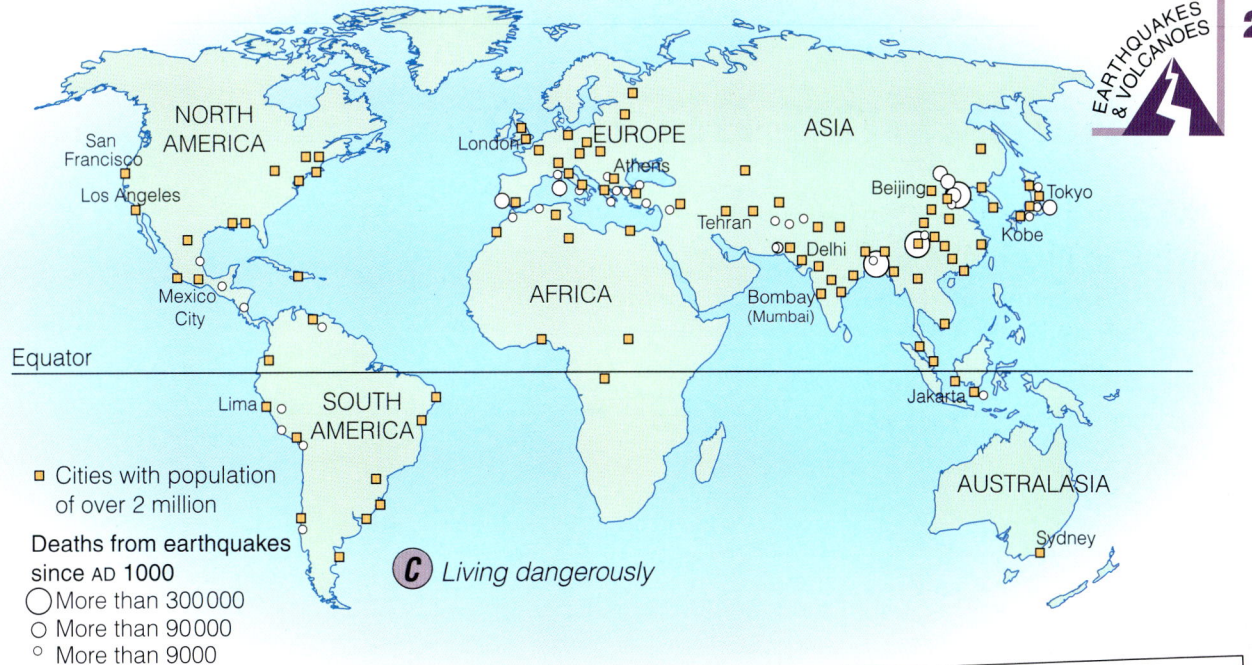

C Living dangerously

- ■ Cities with population of over 2 million

Deaths from earthquakes since AD 1000
- ◯ More than 300 000
- ○ More than 90 000
- ○ More than 9 000

High rise cities in high risk places

More than 100 of the world's cities have over two million people in them. Half of these cities are in, or close to, earthquake zones or volcanoes. What will happen to the people if there are new eruptions and earthquakes?

Violent volcanic eruption predicted

The world is due for a major volcanic eruption according to scientists. Too many volcanoes have been quiet for a long time.

For example, Mount Vesuvius, near Naples in Italy, has not erupted since 1944. Before that, it usually erupted every 20 years.

If Vesuvius erupts, 800 000 people will have to be evacuated.

Mount Vesuvius erupting, 1944

San Francisco waits for the big one: major earthquake predicted before 2000

San Francisco could end the century the way it began, according to scientists. An earthquake more devastating than the big one of 1906 may hit the city before the year 2000.

D Predicting new eruptions and earthquakes

4 a On your map of earthquakes and volcanoes, mark and label the cities named on MAP **C**.
b Which cities are located in an earthquake zone or close to an active volcano?
c List the areas that have had more than 90 000 deaths from earthquakes since AD 1000.

5 Read the extracts in **D**.
a What do scientists predict?
b Suggest why so many people still live in cities like San Francisco and Naples.

6 'Earthquakes and volcanoes can happen anywhere.' Do you think this is true? Give reasons for your answer.

3 | Like biting an apple

**What is the Earth's structure like?
What is its crust like?
How are continents and oceans formed?**

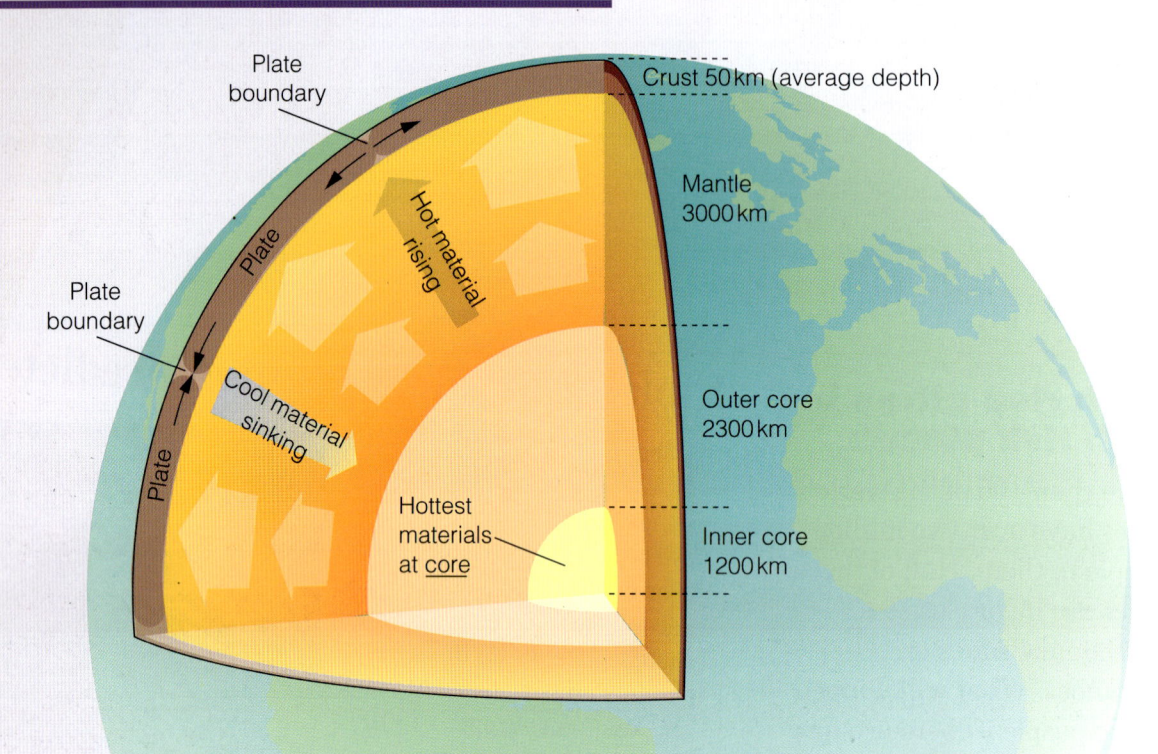

Plate boundary
Crust 50 km (average depth)
Mantle 3000 km
Hot material rising
Plate
Plate boundary
Cool material sinking
Plate
Outer core 2300 km
Hottest materials at <u>core</u>
Inner core 1200 km

A Hot on the inside

Journey to the centre of the Earth

Think of some science fiction stories or films about journeys to the centre of the Earth. When the oldest stories were written, no one knew much about what was below the Earth's surface. Today, scientists know a lot about the inside of the Earth. This is because they study earthquakes and volcanoes which give clues to what is underneath the Earth's <u>crust</u>.

1 Think about when you last bit through an apple.
  How many layers were there? What did you notice about the thickness and texture of each layer?

2 Study DIAGRAM **A**.
  a *On a copy of* DIAGRAM **A** *label:*
  • crust • mantle
  • outer core • inner core.
  b *Add the information about the temperatures of materials.*
  c *Give your diagram a title.*
  d *How many kilometres is it from the surface of the crust to the centre of the Earth?*

70

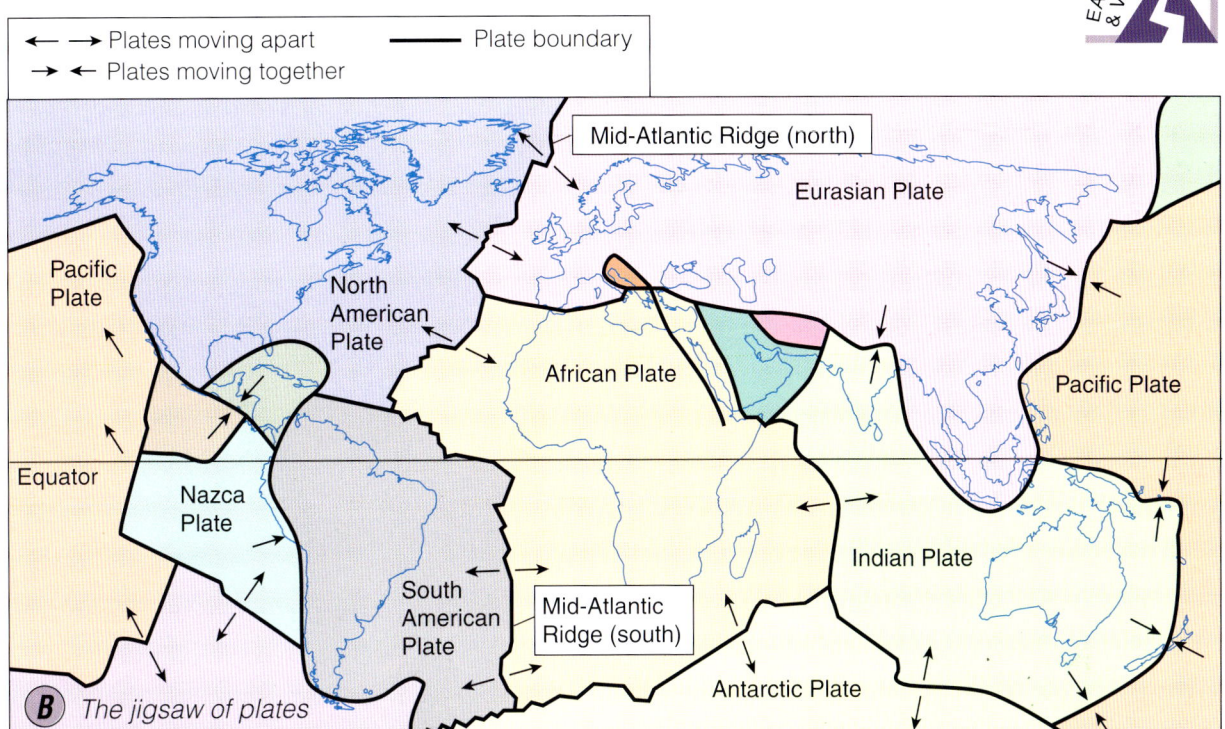

← → Plates moving apart — Plate boundary
→ ← Plates moving together

B *The jigsaw of plates*

Crust broken into plates

MAP **B** shows that the Earth's crust is like a jigsaw. It is broken into great slabs of rock called plates. The plates can move very slowly. Their edges meet at plate boundaries. We find earthquakes and volcanoes at these boundaries.

3 *Study* MAP **B**.
 a *Copy and complete the table below for five named plates. Use an atlas to help.*

Name of plate	Country on the plate
African Plate	Nigeria
Indian Plate	

4 *You need tracing paper or a transparency for this task.*
 a *Trace the plate boundaries from* MAP **B**.
 b *Carefully lay your tracing over* MAP **A** *on page 68.*
 c *Mark on your tracing paper places where the active volcano and earthquake zones match the plate boundaries.*
 d *Name three areas with little risk of earthquakes or eruptions. Use* MAP **B** *to explain your choices.*

5 *Look at* SATELLITE IMAGE **C**.
 a *Describe what the ocean floor looks like.*
 b *Use* MAP **B** *to name the plates on each side of the Mid-Atlantic Ridge. What is happening to them?*

Take Away the Water

What do you think the surface of the Earth looks like without oceans?

Oceans cover more than 70 per cent of the surface of the plates. The highest parts, above the oceans, are called continents. You can see all the surface of each plate when the water is taken away. SATELLITE IMAGE **C** shows you the ocean floor between North America and Europe. This is where two plates meet at the Mid-Atlantic Ridge.

C *Satellite image of the Mid-Atlantic Ridge*

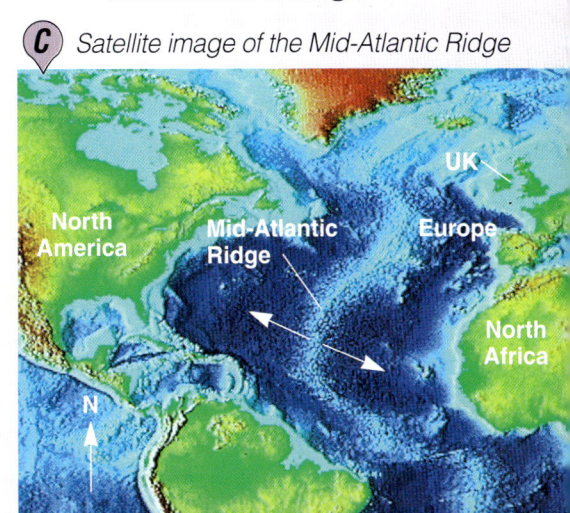

4 | Crust factories

What is a ridge?
What happens at a ridge and why?
How do ridges affect people?

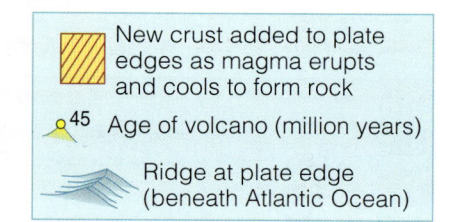

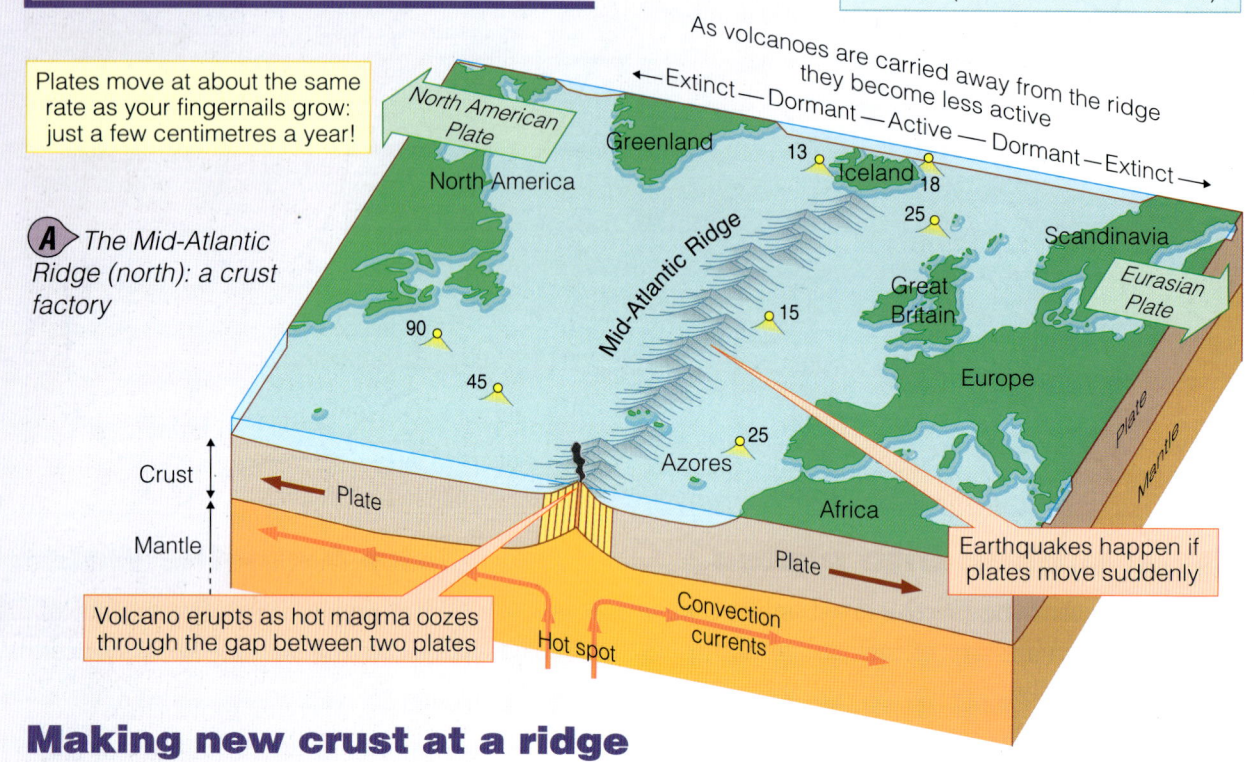

New crust added to plate edges as magma erupts and cools to form rock

○45 Age of volcano (million years)

Ridge at plate edge (beneath Atlantic Ocean)

As volcanoes are carried away from the ridge they become less active
← Extinct — Dormant — Active — Dormant — Extinct →

North American Plate
Greenland
North America
Iceland 13, 18
Scandinavia
25
Mid-Atlantic Ridge
Great Britain 15
Eurasian Plate
90
45
Azores 25
Europe
Africa
Plate
Mantle

Plates move at about the same rate as your fingernails grow: just a few centimetres a year!

A ▷ The Mid-Atlantic Ridge (north): a crust factory

Crust
Mantle
← Plate
Volcano erupts as hot magma oozes through the gap between two plates
Hot spot
Convection currents
Plate →
Earthquakes happen if plates move suddenly

Making new crust at a ridge

What happens when you cut your knee? Blood flows up between the broken skin. When the blood cools, it turns solid. New crust forms in a similar way between the Earth's plates.

These plates float on the liquid <u>mantle</u> like rafts. Parts of the mantle are hotter than other parts. As <u>convection currents</u> rise from a hot spot, they push the plate edges up to form a <u>ridge</u>. These currents then flow through the mantle from hot areas to cooler areas. The mantle moves and pulls the plates apart. The gap between the plates is filled with hot <u>magma</u> from the mantle – just like blood oozing from a cut. The magma cools and forms new crust on each plate edge.

The leaking magma forms volcanoes along the Mid-Atlantic Ridge. These ridge volcanoes have gentle slopes. When they appear above the sea, their tops make gently sloping islands like the Azores.

As the plates move, they also rub against each other. This friction causes earthquakes along the ridge.

---

1 Study DIAGRAM **A**.
  a How do earthquakes happen at a ridge?
  b Where are:
   • the youngest volcanoes and
   • the oldest volcanoes, in relation to the ridge?
  c How does an active volcano become
   • dormant, and
   • extinct?
  d Why does this happen?

2 Explain why we call a ridge a 'crust factory'.

72

Constructive plate boundaries

AZORES

In the islands of the Azores, even the volcanoes are at rest.

Strange as it sounds, the crater of a volcano on the Azores is one of the most peaceful places on Earth. The only disturbance comes from the oars of fishermen. Wherever you go, the volcanic origins of these nine Atlantic islands have created an astonishing variety of natural splendours for your delight. Towering peaks and hidden valleys, deep gorges with spectacular waterfalls, black sea-cliffs and hot sulphur springs. And above all, the flowers: row upon row of vivid blossoms in wild abundance. They cascade down the hillside right to the water's edge – where you can swim from sandy coves or plunge into natural volcanic sea pools. The islands could not be more restful.

B Holiday advertisement for the Azores

3 Look at ADVERT **B**.
  a Find the Azores on DIAGRAM **A** and in an atlas.
  b Describe the location of the Azores in relation to the Mid-Atlantic Ridge.
  c The advert states 'the islands are at rest'. Study DIAGRAM **A**. Do you agree with this? Give reasons for your answer.
  d List the attractions provided by the Azores volcano.

4 Complete a paragraph that begins:'My idea of the perfect holiday would/would not be [delete one] a trip to see one of the Azores volcanoes. This is because…'

5 | Crust bins

What is a trench?
What happens at a trench and why?
How are people affected?

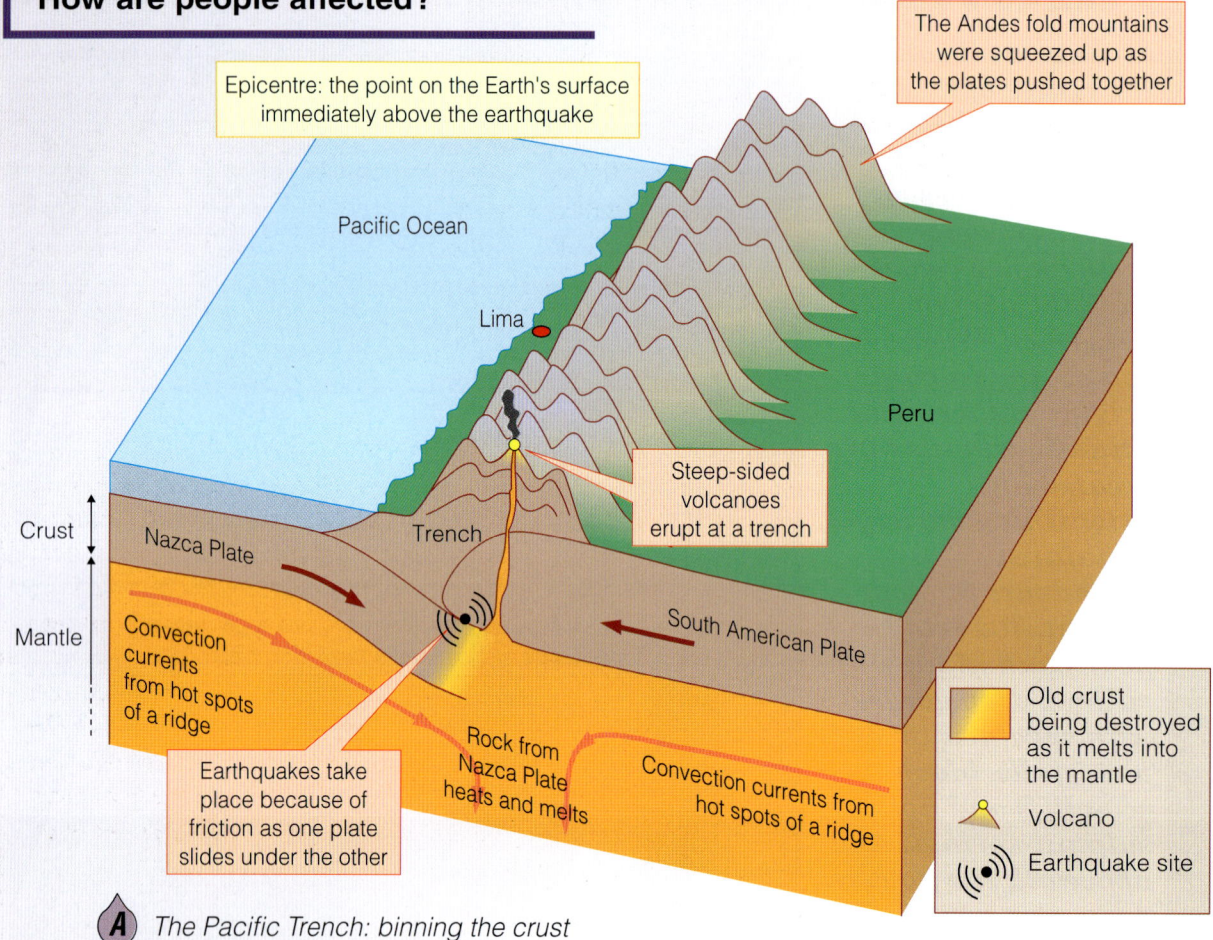

Diagram A labels:
- Epicentre: the point on the Earth's surface immediately above the earthquake
- The Andes fold mountains were squeezed up as the plates pushed together
- Pacific Ocean
- Lima
- Peru
- Steep-sided volcanoes erupt at a trench
- Crust
- Mantle
- Nazca Plate
- Trench
- South American Plate
- Convection currents from hot spots of a ridge
- Rock from Nazca Plate heats and melts
- Convection currents from hot spots of a ridge
- Earthquakes take place because of friction as one plate slides under the other
- Old crust being destroyed as it melts into the mantle
- Volcano
- Earthquake site

A The Pacific Trench: binning the crust

Destroying old crust in a trench

When plates move together, one slides beneath the other. This forms a <u>trench</u>. The front of the plate underneath is melted by the hot mantle. Such melting causes a huge build-up of heat and pressure. This results in earthquakes and volcanic eruptions.

Trench volcanoes erupt very suddenly and violently. They have steeper slopes than ridge volcanoes.

Countries like Peru in South America are close to a trench. Here, the Nazca Plate slides beneath the South American Plate. This means that Peru suffers from earthquakes and volcanoes.

1 Study DIAGRAM **A**.
  a Why is this plate boundary called a trench?
  b How does the shape of a trench volcano differ from a ridge volcano?
  c Name the other landform that has been created at the plate edge. How was it formed?

2 Suggest why we call a trench 'a crust bin'.

Destructive plate boundaries

Miners trapped by earthquake in Peru

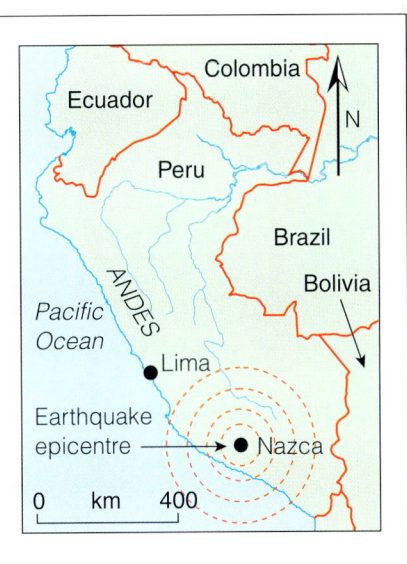

At least 40 gold miners were trapped underground yesterday at a mine high in the Andes. A powerful earthquake measuring 6.4 on the Richter Scale had struck the south coast of Peru. It killed 15 people and injured nearly 700.

The earthquake struck at midday on Tuesday, damaging homes and buildings in Nazca, nearly 400km south-east of Lima, the capital city. An army convoy sent to assist the trapped miners had not reached the site by dawn yesterday. Access roads were blocked by cracks and landslides from the Andes mountains.

A doctor at Nazca hospital said most of the injured were children and elderly people. There were at least two schools damaged. Streets were blocked with rubble and in parts of the city half the homes – simple adobe structures – were damaged.

Doris Flores, who fled her home with her family, said 'We hardly got out when the doorway collapsed. As we were running, the walls from other houses were falling down around us'.

The Times, 16 Nov. 1996

B *An earthquake in the Andes, Peru, 14 November 1996*

---

3 Look at the information in ARTICLE **B**.
  a On what date did the earthquake take place?
  b The Richter Scale measures the strength of earthquakes. What strength did Peru's earthquake measure on the Richter Scale?
  c Use information in **B** and on page 76 to describe what damage you could expect from this earthquake.
  d Describe the location of the earthquake's epicentre in Peru.
  e Why was it difficult for rescue workers to help people in this area?

4 The earthquake hurt many people in this area because they lived in adobe houses.
  a Find out what an adobe house is like.
  b Draw pictures to show how different groups of people were affected by this earthquake.

5 Write a poem or letter about the Peruvian earthquake. Imagine you were one of the following, or another person of your choice:
  - A doctor at the Nazca hospital
  - Doris Flores
  - An 11-year old pupil at the school.

6 | Waiting for the big one!

How do people record earthquakes? Can earthquakes be predicted?

Earthquakes destroy buildings and farmland. Water, gas and electricity services are broken. It may take months for people to repair them. Worst of all, people are killed and homes lost.

Shock waves

If you throw a stone in a pond, ripples spread out. Earthquakes have similar effects. They send out shock waves. We feel these as the ground tremors. Seismologists record them as lines on a seismograph.

A *Shock waves from an earthquake*

B *Seismograph of shock waves from the Maharashtra earthquake, India, 1993*

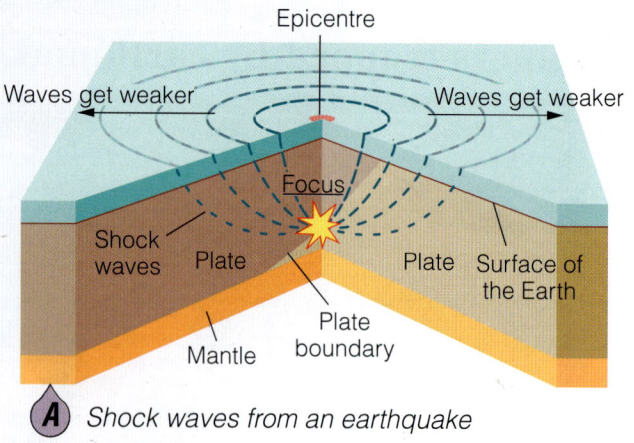

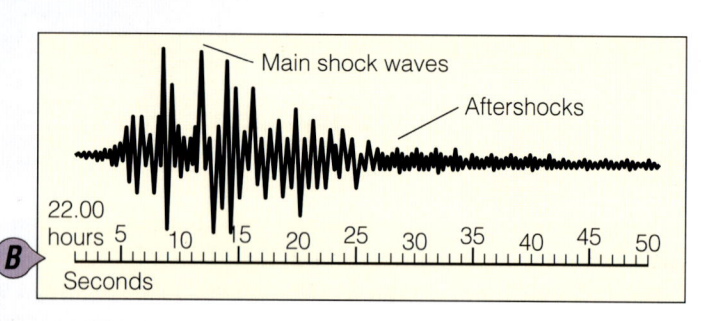

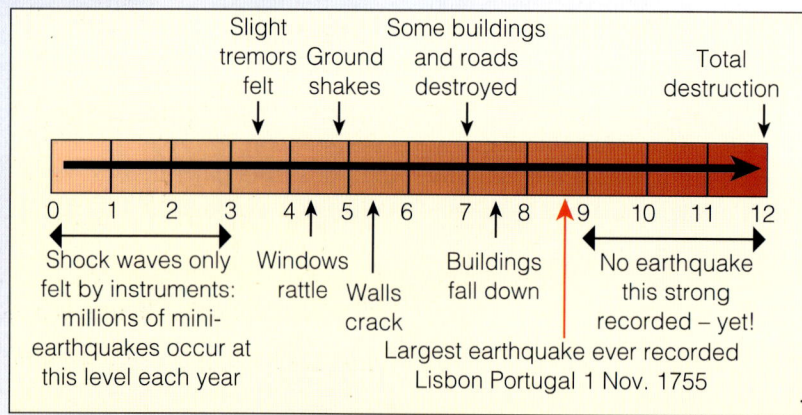

Seismologists also measure the size of earthquakes on a Richter Scale. Soon, seismologists may predict where earthquakes will take place and so warn of danger.

C *The Richter Scale*

1 a Copy DIAGRAM A.
 b Copy and complete the following paragraph.
  An earthquake sends out _____ _____. These get _____ as they travel away from the earthquake. The place where the earthquake happens, below the surface, is called the _____. The place above this, at the surface of the Earth, is called the _____.
 c Use this information to explain how we can detect earthquakes a long way from where they take place.

2 Look at SEISMOGRAPH B. This recording of the Maharashtra earthquake was made in Edinburgh.
 a How many seconds did this earthquake last?
 b When were the largest waves recorded?

3 Study the information in SCALE C.
 a At what strength on the scale can you feel slight tremors?
 b Where was the strongest earthquake ever?
 c How strong was this on the scale?

6

Parkfield predicts!

Parkfield Village claims to be the 'earthquake capital of the world'

Parkfield lies on the San Andreas Fault in California, USA. At this plate boundary two plates slide sideways against each other. This causes frequent earthquakes around Parkfield. Here, scientists check the Earth's movement. They can then predict future earthquakes.

D *The San Andreas Fault, California*

1. Seismometer records small shakes
2. Seismometer records large shakes
3. Creepmeter checks changes where plates meet
4. Strainmeter checks changes in ground shape
5. Sensors check changes in water level
6. Satellite sends information to United States Geological Survey
7. Laser sends beams to reflectors to check movement

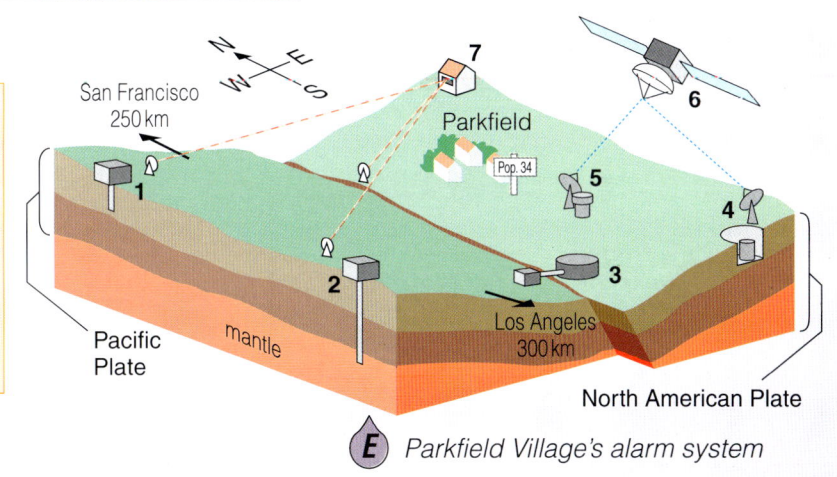

E *Parkfield Village's alarm system*

4 Study PHOTO **D**.

a How can you tell this is a plate boundary?

b Draw your own rough sketch of PHOTO **D** and label which plate is moving north, and which plate is moving south. Give your sketch a title.

c Which two American cities lie alongside this plate boundary?

d Would you agree that people 'live dangerously' in California? Explain your answer.

5 Look at DIAGRAM **E**.

a Copy and complete a table like the one below.

Instrument	Where is it?	What does it do?
1 Seismometer A	NW of Parkfield	Records small shakes
2 Seismometer B		

b What do scientists hope this alarm system will do?

77

7 While a country slept...

What happened at Kobe in 1995?
What did the earthquake do to people and the environment?

What happened?

On 17 January 1995 a huge earthquake struck the town of Kobe in Japan. Look back at the photo on page 65 which shows some damage. Heather Marsden, an English teacher, was there.

My alarm clock was set for 6 o'clock on the morning of Tuesday 17 January. When I set it the night before I had never imagined that, 15 minutes before it rang, I would be jerked awake by a violent shuddering and terrifying rumble. An earthquake!

A What was it like for Heather Marsden?

Total chaos in Kobe

Many people ran from buildings. They were killed by falling debris. Survivors wandered the streets in pyjamas. Fire and police authorities could not cope. Over 5000 people died, and 250 000 were made homeless.

B Danger to people

Elegant city destroyed

Japan's international port, Kobe city, was destroyed by an earthquake this morning. Old wooden buildings fell down causing fire. Even buildings built to cope with shock waves toppled. Modern office blocks, a seven-storey hospital and highways all collapsed.

C Damage in Kobe

1 Read Heather's comments in **A**.
   a For what time was Heather's alarm clock set?
   b At what time did the earthquake happen?
   c What made Heather think it was an earthquake?

2 Read EXTRACTS **B** and **C**.
   Draw some pictures to show how the earthquake affected:
   • people, • the environment.

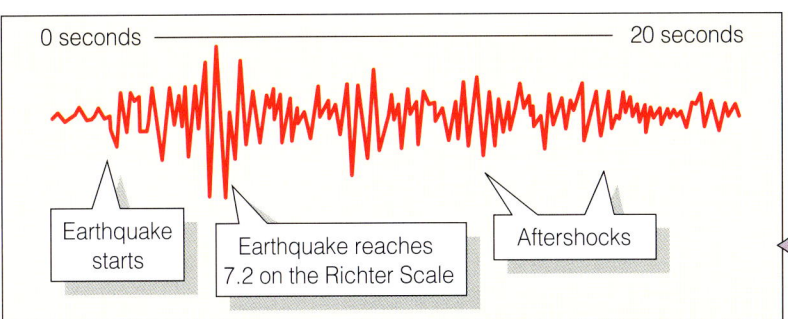

D Seismograph of Kobe earthquake, measured in Dundee, UK

Labels on seismograph: "Earthquake starts", "Earthquake reaches 7.2 on the Richter Scale", "Aftershocks"

What damage did the earthquake do?

Although the earthquake only lasted 20 seconds it did a great deal of damage in Kobe. The earthquake's shock waves affected areas over 100 km away.

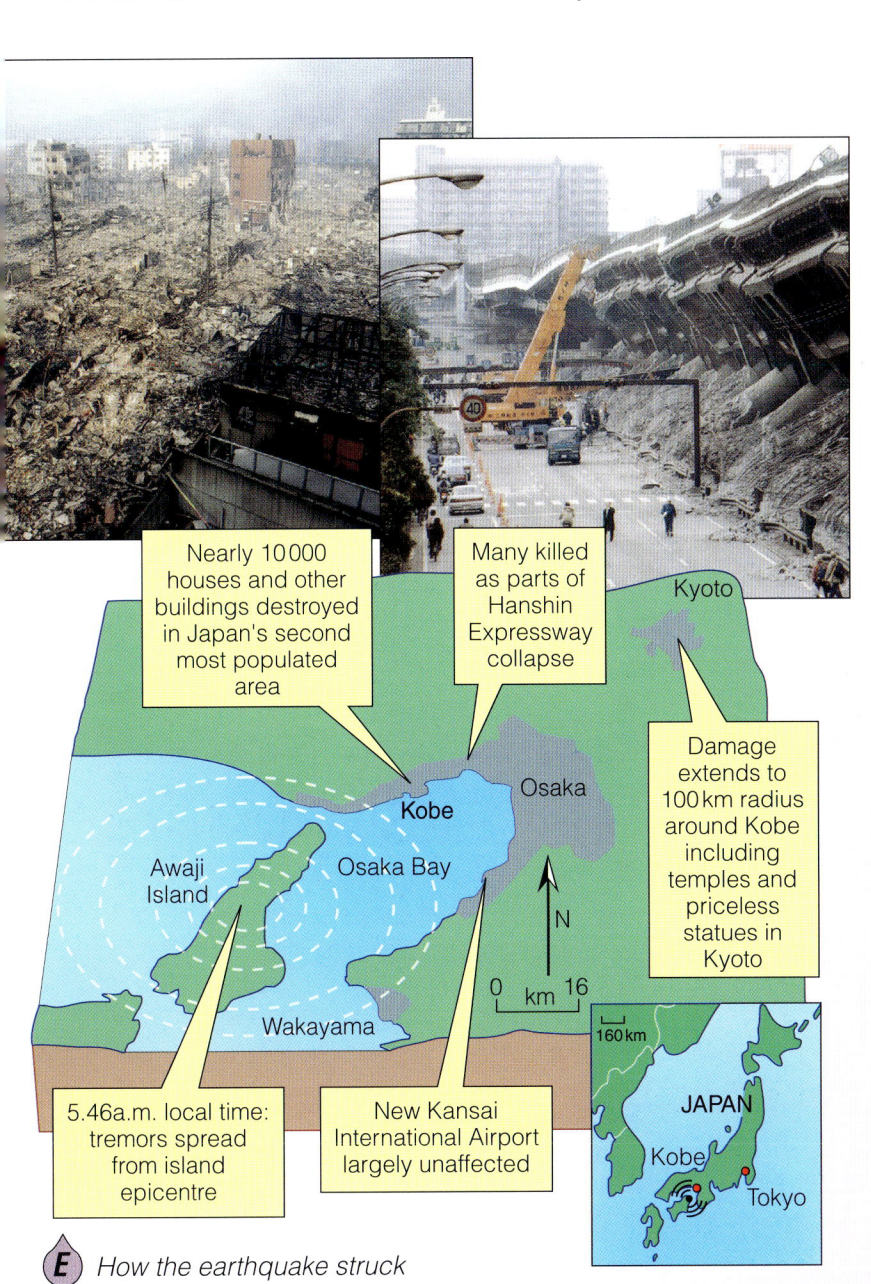

E How the earthquake struck

Map labels:
- Nearly 10 000 houses and other buildings destroyed in Japan's second most populated area
- Many killed as parts of Hanshin Expressway collapse
- Damage extends to 100 km radius around Kobe including temples and priceless statues in Kyoto
- 5.46 a.m. local time: tremors spread from island epicentre
- New Kansai International Airport largely unaffected

Places shown: Kyoto, Osaka, Kobe, Osaka Bay, Awaji Island, Wakayama, Japan, Tokyo

3 Look at SEISMOGRAPH **D**.
  a Where was it recorded?
  b How long did the shock waves last?
  c How large was the earthquake on the Richter Scale?
  d What damage would you expect to see?

4 Study MAP **E**.
  a Where was the epicentre?
  b How far away from Kobe was the epicentre?
  c Describe the distribution of the damage in relation to the epicentre. Refer to distance and direction.

5 Imagine you were stationed in Kobe as a radio news reporter when the earthquake struck. You are ringing the news office to tell them about the earthquake.

You have two minutes to report on the earthquake for the news programmes. What will you say?

8 | Earthquakes: Why Japan?

**Why do earthquakes take place in Japan?
How can Japan limit damage to people and cities?**

Was the Kobe earthquake expected?

Japan has a long history of earthquakes and volcanic eruptions. The country has had to cope with danger for centuries. Instead of moving away from the islands, the people of Japan try to build their cities to avoid damage.

Many of Japan's earthquakes take place under the Pacific Ocean. Not all earthquakes cause death and damage, so they do not make the news. In January 1995 three large earthquakes hit Japan, but in the UK we only heard about Kobe.

Date	Richter Scale measurement	Location of epicentre	Damage
1923	7.9 (est.)	In Sagami Bay just off Honshu coast	'The Great Kanti earthquake' was Japan's worst ever: • Tokyo completely destroyed • 140 000 people killed • 50 000 wooden buildings collapsed • Damage by fire and tidal waves
1 January 1995	6.7	Beneath sea off east coast of Honshu	• Little damage
7 January 1995	6.9	Beneath sea off east coast of Honshu	• Little damage
17 January 1995	7.2	Epicentre close to densely populated city of Kobe	• 6300 people killed • 25 000 people injured • 56 000 buildings damaged • 50 000 people remained homeless 2 years later

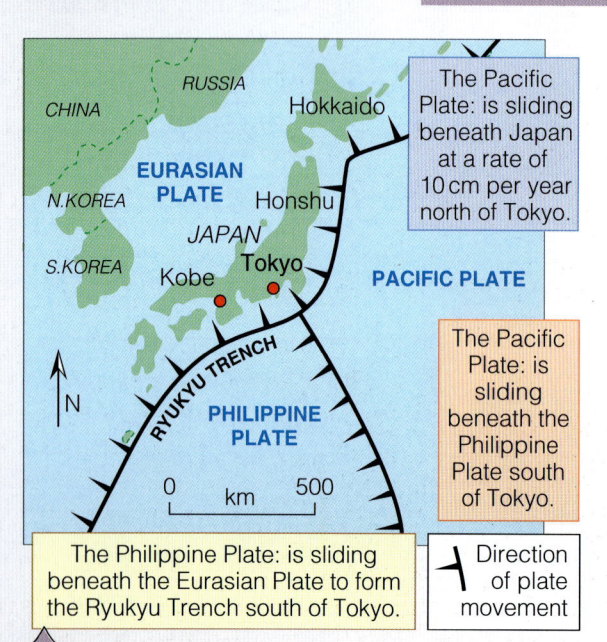

A Some of Japan's many earthquakes

B Japan lies near plate boundaries

- The Pacific Plate: is sliding beneath Japan at a rate of 10 cm per year north of Tokyo.
- The Pacific Plate: is sliding beneath the Philippine Plate south of Tokyo.
- The Philippine Plate: is sliding beneath the Eurasian Plate to form the Ryukyu Trench south of Tokyo.

1 Use the text and TABLE **A**.
  a Describe the damage caused by Japan's worst earthquake.
  b Where did other Japanese earthquakes take place in Japan in 1995?
  c Why do some Japanese earthquakes not make international news?

2 Look at MAP **B**. Add all the labels to a copy of MAP **B**.

3 a On which plate is Kobe?
  b Which two plates are pushing towards Japan?
  c Which plate movement caused the earthquake? Explain how.

Protecting the people

Japan works hard to protect its people from earthquakes. Japanese cities are the safest in the world but they still need to be made safer.

Earthquake-proof building, Tokyo

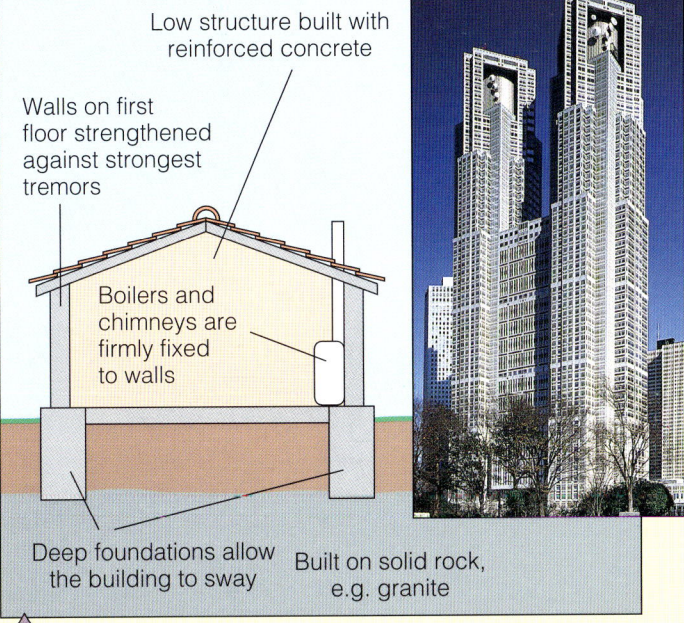

Practising earthquake drill, Japan

Low structure built with reinforced concrete

Walls on first floor strengthened against strongest tremors

Boilers and chimneys are firmly fixed to walls

Deep foundations allow the building to sway

Built on solid rock, e.g. granite

C *Protection from earthquake damage*

4 a Make a list of what you do during your school's fire drill.
 b Look at how the Japanese protect themselves from earthquakes in PHOTO **c** above.
 c Make another list of what you would need to do during an earthquake.
 d Compare your lists. How are they different? Why?

5 Study PHOTO **D**.
 a How quickly after the earthquake was the Hanshin Expressway bridge repaired?
 b What has been done to make it safer?
 c Why do you think the Expressway was mended so quickly?

6 You have entered a competition. You have to give advice to the Chief Planner of a new town. She has to design buildings and bridges that will limit earthquake damage. Prepare your entry using information from these pages.

Making the bridge safe:
- arched steel plates make the bridge much stronger
- concrete pillars are now 60 cm wider than before
- a rubber layer between the pillars and bridge surface helps absorb shock waves

D *Repairing the damage: the bridge of the Hanshin Expressway linking Kobe and Osaka was re-opened on 30 September 1996*

9 Where will the next volcano erupt?

Can scientists predict volcanic eruptions? Where do we measure volcanic activity?

> At 200 m down, the last of the light faded away. The temperature had dropped sharply from the 33°C at the surface. The pressure outside was over 300 times what we have on land. Our spotlight picked out the mountains of the Mid-Atlantic Ridge. They were surrounded by thousands of shrimps!

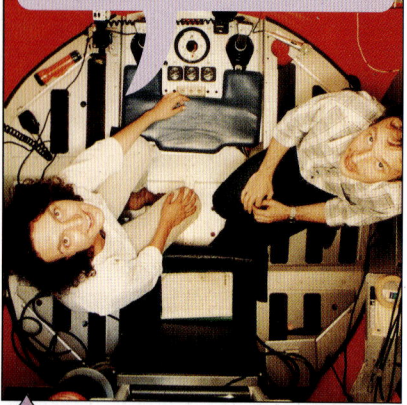

In the last 20 years, only 25 000 people have been killed by volcanoes erupting. This is very few deaths compared to earthquakes. But volcanoes can damage areas far away. This is because they make dust, smoke and ash. These stay in the <u>atmosphere</u> and can change our weather. We need to find out when volcanoes may erupt.

Going down!

We cannot stop volcanoes erupting but <u>vulcanologists</u> are getting better at predicting volcanic activity. One way is by exploring plate boundaries deep beneath oceans.

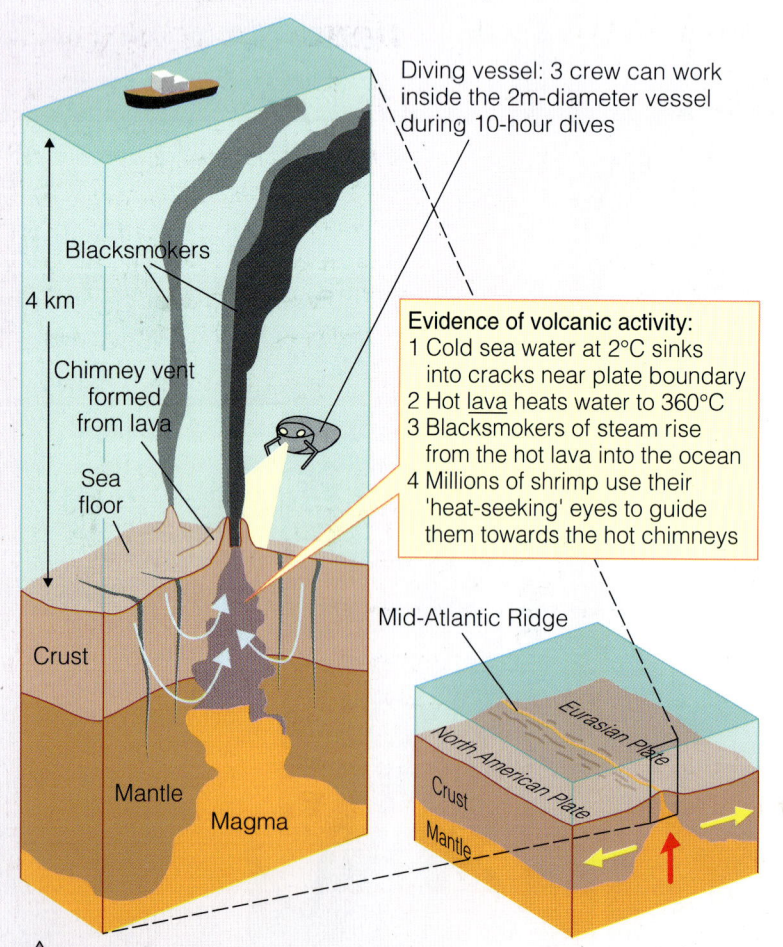

A Vulcanologist Dr Mills and a scientist preparing for their deep-sea expedition, October 1994

Diving vessel: 3 crew can work inside the 2m-diameter vessel during 10-hour dives

Blacksmokers
4 km
Chimney vent formed from lava
Sea floor
Crust
Mantle
Magma
Mid-Atlantic Ridge
Eurasian Plate
North American Plate
Crust
Mantle

Evidence of volcanic activity:
1 Cold sea water at 2°C sinks into cracks near plate boundary
2 Hot <u>lava</u> heats water to 360°C
3 Blacksmokers of steam rise from the hot lava into the ocean
4 Millions of shrimp use their 'heat-seeking' eyes to guide them towards the hot chimneys

B How scientists know there is volcanic activity at the Mid-Atlantic Ridge

---

1 Read about Dr Mills' JOURNEY **A**.
  a Explain why scientists are exploring the ocean depths.
  b Imagine exploring the ocean bed with Dr Mills. Produce a storyboard to illustrate your journey. Add some ideas of your own to describe what it might be like.

2 Study the DIAGRAMS in **B**. Produce a leaflet with the title 'Not many people know this ... about volcanoes' Your leaflet needs to be in three parts:
  1 How scientists are exploring the ocean bed.
  2 What they are looking for.
  3 How this helps them predict where volcanoes may erupt.

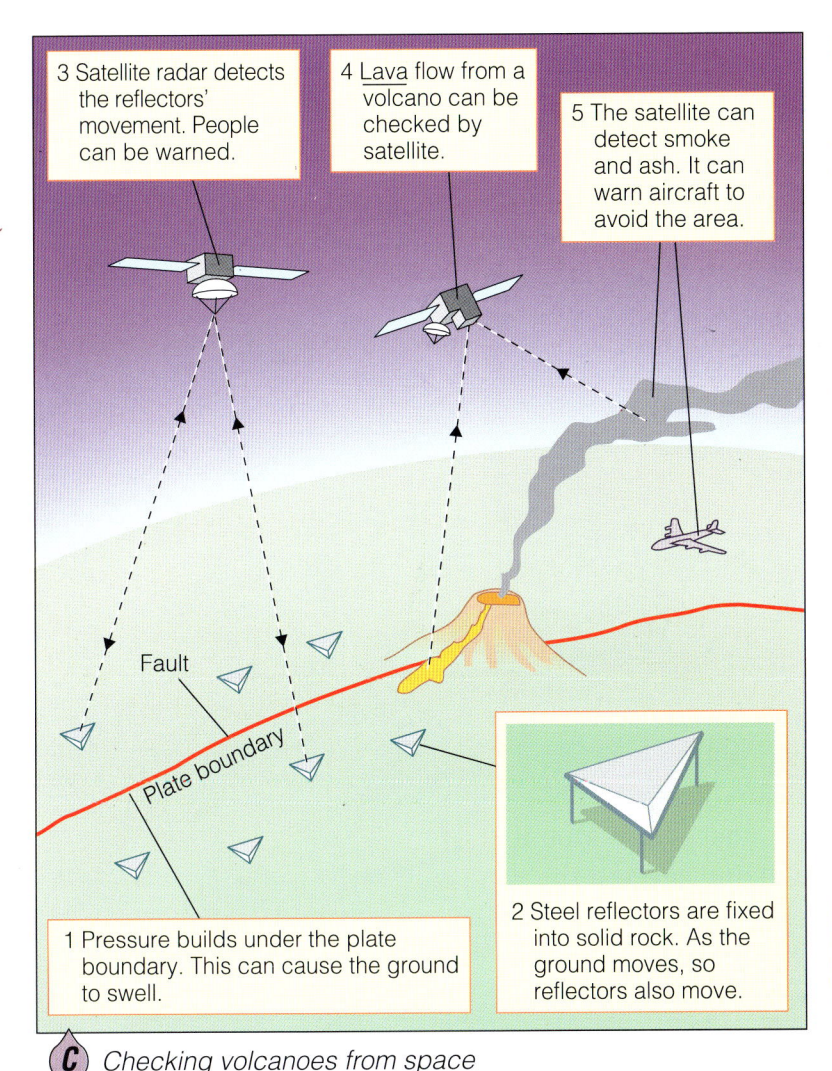

High in the sky

Before volcanoes erupt, the earth's surface may swell up. This is caused by pressure underground. Few people live on volcano slopes, so this swelling is not always noticed – until it is too late! But <u>satellites</u> can detect ground-swelling. They can warn us of an eruption.

Diagram C – Checking volcanoes from space:

1. Pressure builds under the plate boundary. This can cause the ground to swell.
2. Steel reflectors are fixed into solid rock. As the ground moves, so reflectors also move.
3. Satellite radar detects the reflectors' movement. People can be warned.
4. <u>Lava</u> flow from a volcano can be checked by satellite.
5. The satellite can detect smoke and ash. It can warn aircraft to avoid the area.

June 1982

Java eruption almost blows plane out of sky

A British Airways plane and its 247 passengers almost fell out of the sky when there was a sudden volcanic eruption. The cabin was filled with smoke and its engines were clogged with ash...

D Danger to planes

---

3 Look at DIAGRAM **C**.
  a Where are the reflectors fixed?
  b Suggest why they are on both sides of the plate boundary.
  c Copy and complete the table to show what comes out of a volcano.

	Material erupted	Where material moves
1	Ash	Air
2	Lava	
3		

4 a Use ARTICLE **D** to explain what happened over Java.
  b How might satellites have helped to prevent this?

5 'Trying to predict the next volcanic eruption is a waste of money. There is nothing we can do to stop it.'
  a To what extent do you agree with this view?
  b Compare your views with others in your class.

10 No skiing today: Eruption in progress

Where did the Mount Ruapehu volcano erupt?
What came out of the volcano?
What damage did it cause?

Mud and ash

Few people are killed by volcanoes. It is difficult to build houses on the steep slopes of volcanoes, so not many people live there. Unlike sudden earthquakes, volcanoes usually give warning signs. People can escape.

All of New Zealand's active volcanoes are on North Island. In June 1996, just as the ski season was about to start, disaster hit. A huge lahar (mudflow with hot water and ash) swept down the ski slopes from Mount Ruapehu. Then the volcano erupted and covered the snowy mountain with black ash. The ski season was postponed until August and finished in September.

A New Zealand

B Smoke and ash billow from Mount Ruapehu

C Many materials come out of an erupting volcano

Monday 17 June 1996

am
- Lahars flow down the Tukino ski field and Whangaehu river valley.
- Mt Ruapehu erupts.
- Ash plume rises to 12 km – seen from Palmerston. Ash spread by south-west winds up to 100 km around the volcano. Ash falls as far north as Tauranga and as far east as Whakatane.

pm
- Heavy ash falls in Lake Taupo region. People advised to stay indoors and seal water tanks against falling ash.
- Ash 'falls like snow' in Rotorua to form a layer 1 cm thick.
- Ash covers all slopes of Mt Tongarino, Mt Ngauruhoe and Mt Ruapehu.
- Mt Ruapehu continues to explode.

pm
- The earth shakes. Rocks and ash glow in the sky and land over 1 km away.

Tuesday 18 June 1996
- Volcanic activity falls to only 10% of yesterday.
- Sticky black substance falls in Taupo: it doesn't brush off.
- Ash layer covers most of Whakapapa ski field. Skiers called in after two hours of training.
- Motorists advised to change air filters and oil as ash can destroy engines.
- Volcanic activity dies out through the day.

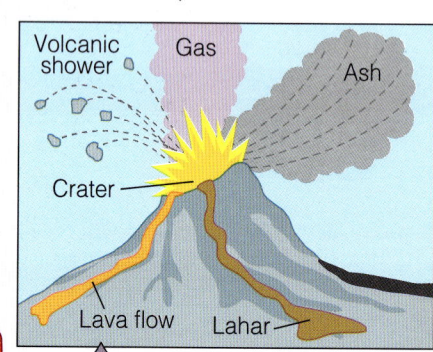

D Diary of Mount Ruapehu's eruption

1 Study MAP A.
  a How many large islands make up New Zealand?
  b On which island is Mount Ruapehu?
  c Compare its height to that of Mount Cook on South Island.

2 a When is the ski season on Mt Ruapehu?
  b Explain why it is in these months.
  c What stopped the skiing?

10 EARTHQUAKES & VOLCANOES

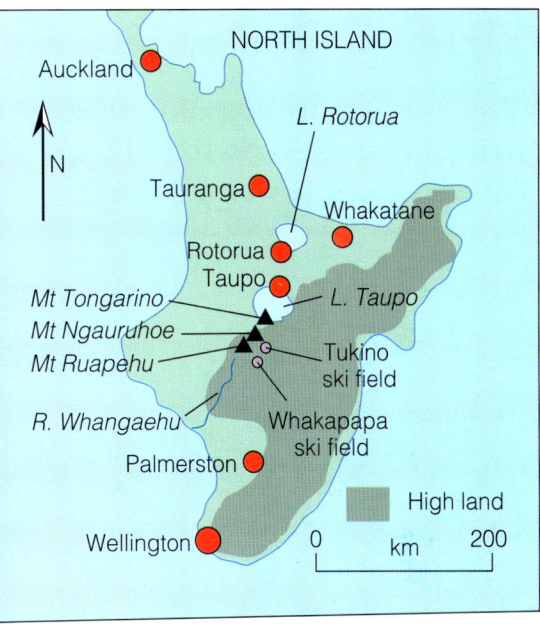

What damage took place? **E**

Rocks larger than cars!

Residents are staying indoors in towns near Mt Ruapehu. Rocks the size of cars have been landing up to 1 km away from the volcano. Ash covers buildings and roads. A thick black cloud of smoke and gas blocks the sun. In Rotorua, 120 km north, the touring Scottish rugby side cancelled its training. Eight airports within 160 km of the volcano are closed. Flights are cancelled for 3000 passengers. It is feared that the ash may clog engines. The cost in lost income for ski resorts and hotels is about £4.5 million although visitors are coming to watch the volcano!

The Times 18 June 1996

---

3 a Draw DIAGRAM **C**.

b Write these sentences in the correct place on your diagram:
- Hot lava flows out of the volcano along the ground.
- Huge rocks blasted into the air can travel several kilometres.
- This can poison people and wildlife.
- This rises to damage aircraft and can settle over large areas of land.

4 Use your diagram and DIARY **D**.

a Which materials on your diagram came out of Mount Ruapehu?

b On an outline map of North Island mark on the places mentioned in DIARY **D**. Use MAP **E** to help.

c Show where ash, rocks and lahars went. Use different colours for each and add a key.

5 Study the information in **E**.

a Describe what the person is doing. Explain why.

b Use **E** and other sources to list the effects of the eruption. Write about: • people, • the environment, • the economy.

6 Look at PHOTO **B** and the photo on page 65. Imagine you were on the ski slopes when Mount Ruapehu erupted. Design a postcard to send to a friend in the UK. You need a picture and a message of no more than 30 words.

85

11 | Volcanoes: Why North Island?

Why did Mount Ruapehu erupt?
What can people do to limit damage?
Why do tourists come here?

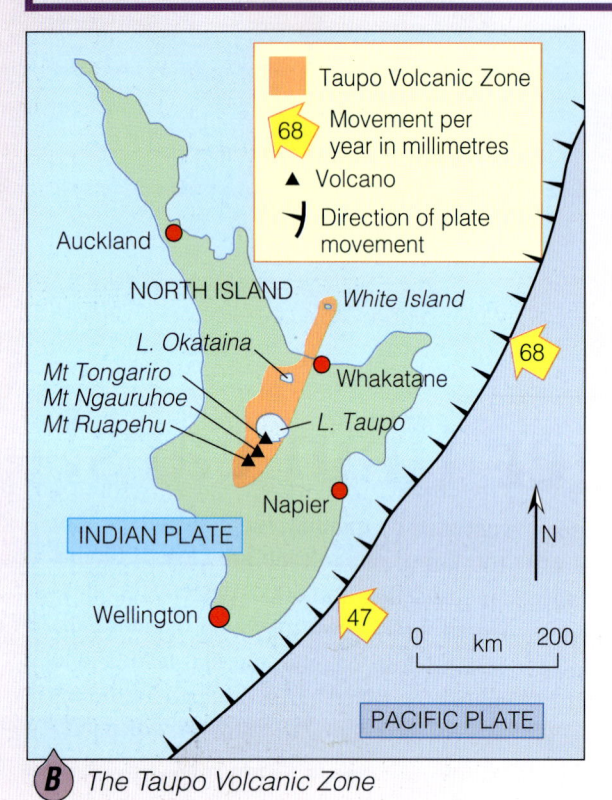

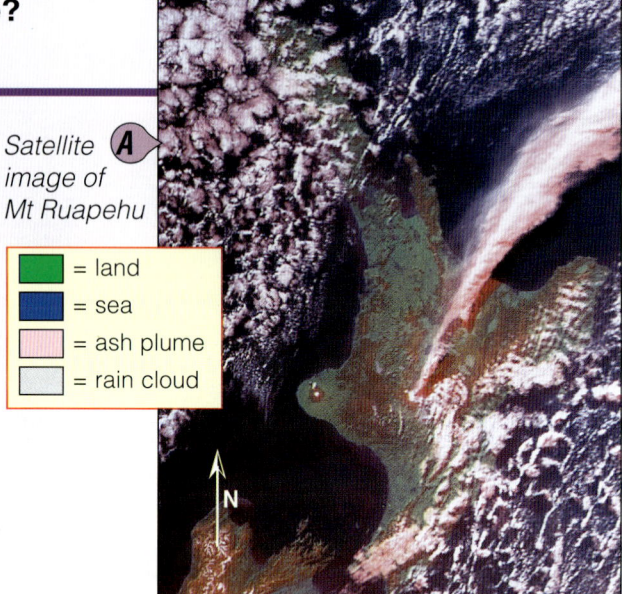

B The Taupo Volcanic Zone

Satellite image of Mt Ruapehu **A**

= land
= sea
= ash plume
= rain cloud

Spy in the sky

Mount Ruapehu began to erupt early in the morning of 17 June 1996. That afternoon, at 3.00 p.m., a Japanese satellite recorded IMAGE **A**. It shows an ash plume rising up 20 km above North Island.

1 Look at IMAGE **A**.
   a Locate the ash plume over North Island. In which direction is it blowing?
   b Which direction is the wind blowing from?
   c Suggest what problems the ash caused at this height.
   d Compare IMAGE **A** with MAP **B**. Identify areas and towns affected by the ash. Suggest some problems people may have suffered there.

2 Study MAP **B**.
   a On which plate is Mount Ruapehu?
   b List the other volcanoes on North Island.
   c Which plate is moving towards North Island? How fast?
   d Describe the location of the Taupo Volcanic Zone. Include: • position on North Island, • position of volcanoes, • relationship to plates.

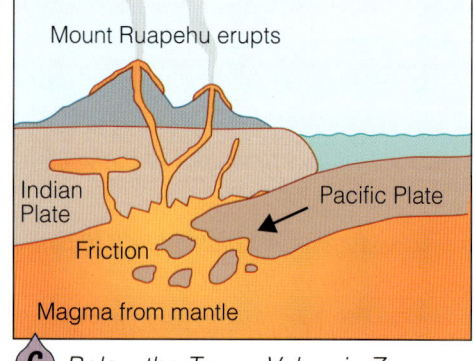

C Below the Taupo Volcanic Zone

3 Look at DIAGRAM **C**.
   a Is this plate boundary a trench or a ridge? Explain your answer.
   b North Island also suffers from earthquakes. Explain why.

Don't panic!

People cannot stop volcanic eruptions. But scientists can check on earth movements and warn us when an eruption might happen.

4 Study the advice in **D**.
  a Think of more advice which might help protect people during an eruption.
  b Produce a more effective poster with some illustrations.
  c Explain how your poster could reduce danger to people both indoors and outdoors.

Stay indoors
Close doors and windows
Save some water

If you have to leave your home…

Wear heavy clothing over your head and body
Breathe through a handkerchief or wet cloth
Carry a torch

D What to do in an eruption!

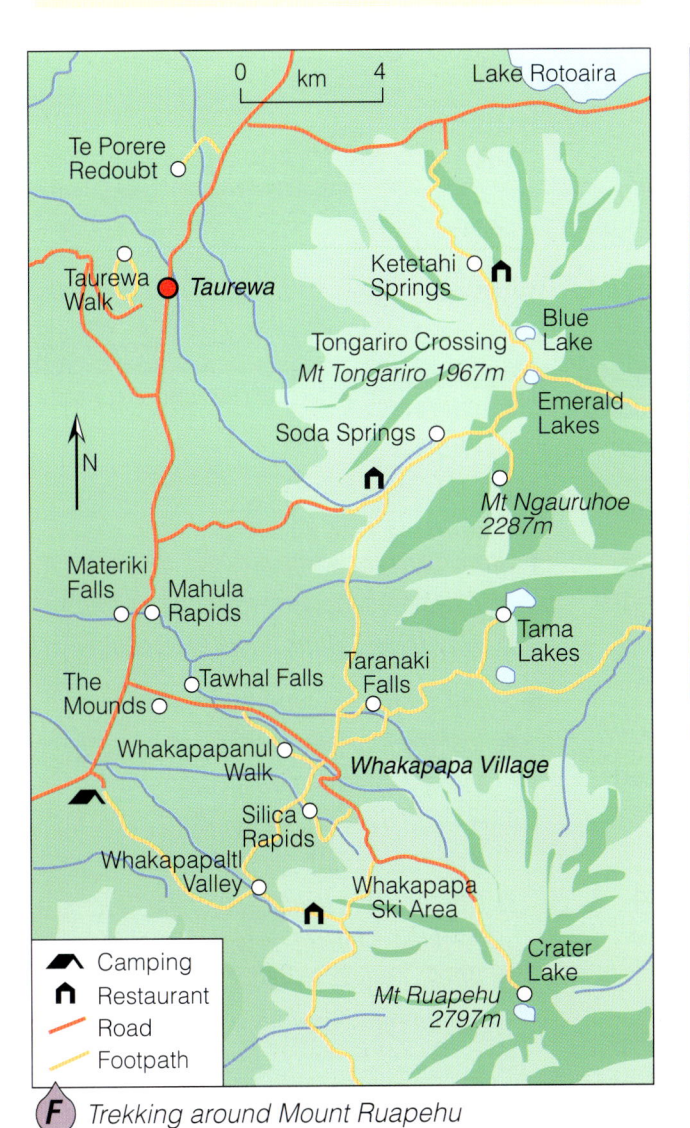

E Watching a volcano in the Taupo Zone

5 North Island's volcanoes are dangerous, but they still attract many walkers. Study MAP **F**.
  a Describe a route walking from Lake Rotoaira to Mt Ruapehu. Choose any route that uses roads and marked paths.
  b Draw a plan of your route. Add a key, scale and a north pointer.

F Trekking around Mount Ruapehu

12 | Volcanoes in Britain!

Where is there evidence of volcanic activity in Britain?
What are volcanic landforms?
How do people use volcanic landforms?

Giant's Causeway (basalt)

Wicklow Mountains

Edinburgh Castle

Dartmoor (granite)

Key:
- Intrusive igneous rocks
- Extrusive igneous rocks

A *Evidence of volcanic activity in Britain*

Upland and lowland Britain

Britain is made up of different rocks. There are hard and soft rocks. Upland Britain has many hard rocks. Some of these are called <u>igneous rocks</u>.

Some igneous rocks formed as lava erupted out of a volcano on to the Earth's surface. These are called <u>extrusive rocks</u>. The best known is basalt. Other igneous rocks formed when magma cooled underground. These are called <u>intrusive rocks</u>. We see these on the Earth's surface only after <u>erosion</u> uncovers them. The best known is granite.

---

1 Study SATELLITE IMAGE **A**.
  a What does the Tees–Exe line divide?
  b Why do you think it has this name?

2 Study the photos around IMAGE **A**.
  a List the four places in the photos. Use the key to decide which are:
    • extrusive igneous rocks
    • intrusive igneous rocks.
  b Compare the landscape in the Wicklow Mountains with Dartmoor.
  c What use was made of igneous rock in Edinburgh? Suggest why.
  d Suggest why the Giant's Causeway has this name.

12 EARTHQUAKES & VOLCANOES

3 Use an outline copy of DIAGRAM **B**. Add the correct labels to each of the landforms shown. Refer to this label box or use your own words.

- Lava flows on to the surface. It cools down to make extrusive rocks.
- Magma flows between rock layers underground. It makes intrusive rocks.
- A large crater lake may form in a caldera.
- A caldera is a volcano that has had its cone blown off.
- Hot magma from the mantle.
- Ash showers cover the countryside.
- When exposed, an old volcanic plug makes a good base for a castle.
- Each eruption gives out ash. This settles on top of lava.

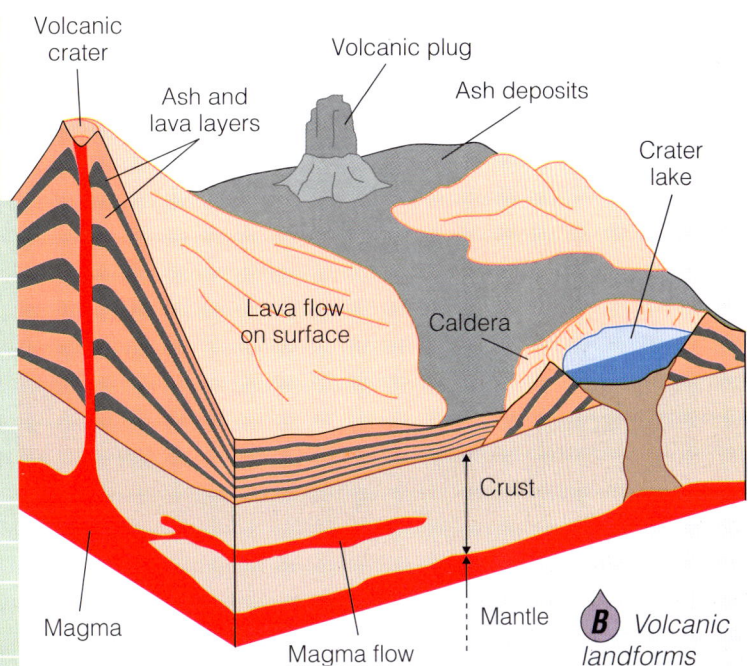

B Volcanic landforms

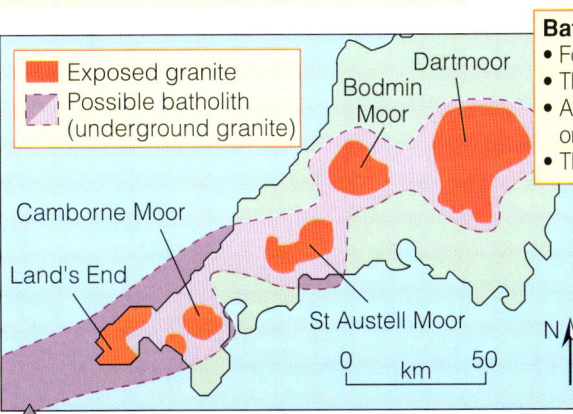

C Below Devon and Cornwall

Batholiths
- Formed when magma cooled underground.
- This made a huge mountain of granite (batholith) below the ground.
- After millions of years, <u>weathering</u> and erosion wear away the rocks on top of the batholith.
- The batholith is then exposed at the surface.

4 Study MAP **C**.
  a List the following exposed granite areas in order from west to east: Dartmoor, St Austell Moor, Camborne Moor, Land's End, Bodmin Moor.
  b What is a moor? Suggest why the granite is mostly left as moorland.
  c How does the map suggest that the moors are just the tops of a single batholith?

5 Look at MAP **D**.
  a List some different land-uses that take place on each of the granite moorlands named in MAP **C**.
  b 'The granite moorlands of Cornwall and Devon are of no use to people.' Do you agree with this statement? Explain your answer.

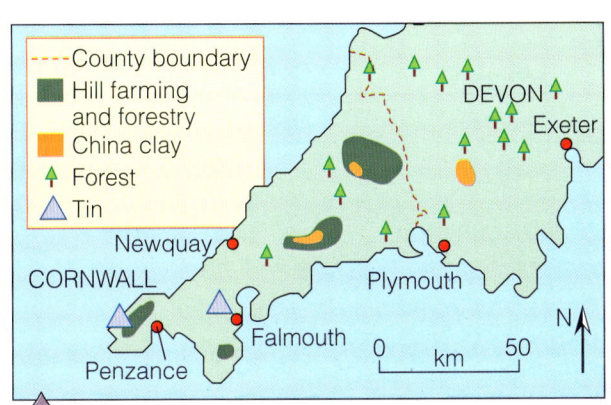

D What use are granite areas?

89

13 | Just when you thought it was safe…

Why are there small earthquakes in Britain? What damage might a large earthquake cause?

- ● Earthquake high-risk area
- ○ Earthquake sites since 1700

Inverness: hit by earthquakes in 1769, 1816, 1888 and 1901.

London: plate movements under the Strait of Dover have shaken SE England every 200 years. Although quiet since 1776, another shake is due.

Hereford: hit by tremors in 1863, 1896 and 1926.

Swansea: weak rocks lie underneath. The last big tremor was in 1906.

Strait of Dover

Colchester: In 1884 Britain's worst earthquake killed 4 people. It destroyed the church spire and damaged 1200 houses.

British Geological Survey

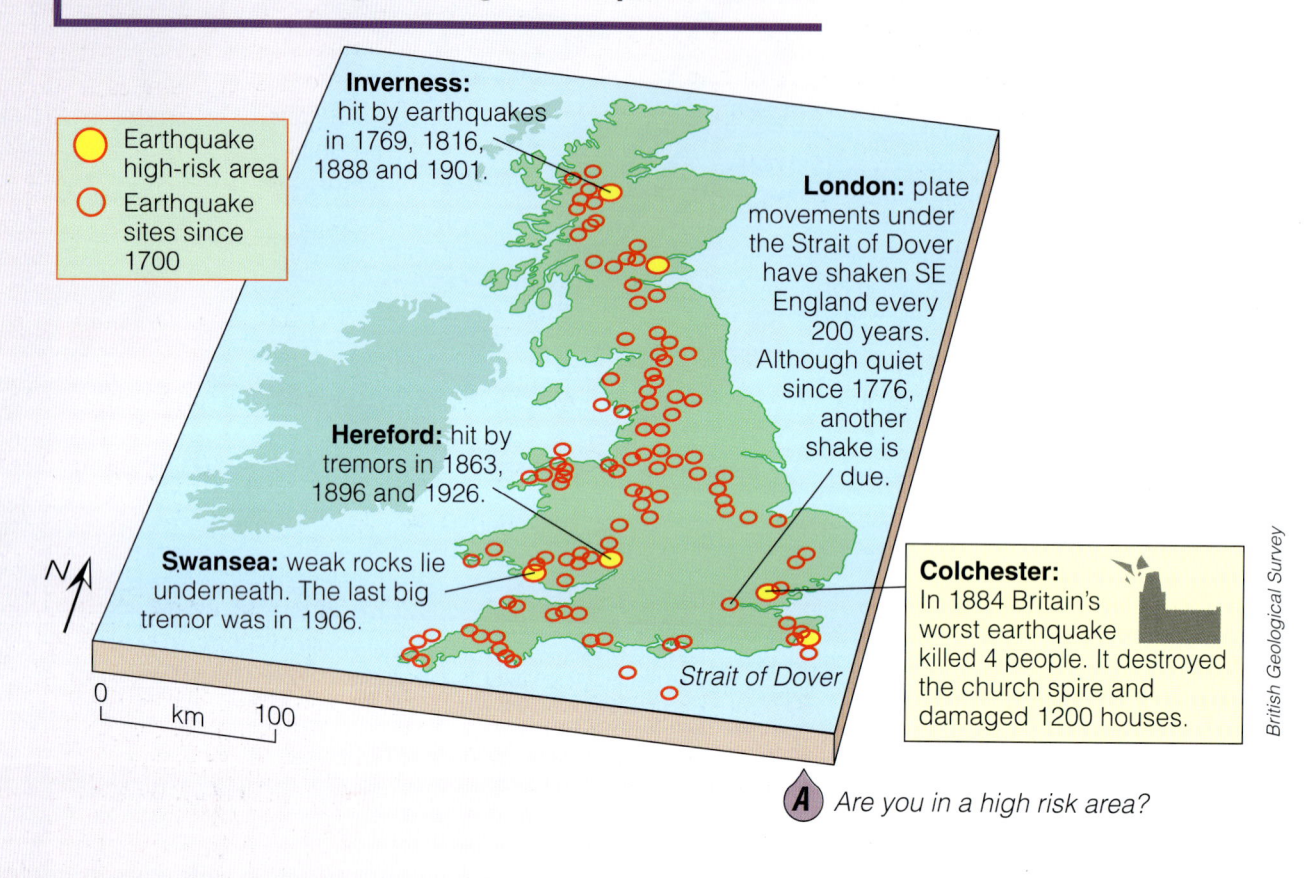

A Are you in a high risk area?

Plate movements affect Britain

Britain was once closer to a plate boundary. Over millions of years, the rocks making up Britain moved east of the Mid-Atlantic Ridge. Today, Britain lies on the Eurasian Plate – far away from a plate boundary. There should be no volcanic eruptions here now.

But when plate boundaries move, there are vibrations. These may spread across plates and cause minor shakes in some parts of Britain.

1 a Use the information around MAP **A** to complete a table like the one below. Put the earthquakes in date order. The first one has been done. Add the title: 'A diary of Britain's earthquakes since 1700'.

Year	Location	Comment
1769	Inverness	Has had 4 since 1700

b Where and when was Britain's worst earthquake? List the damage it caused to people and the environment.

c Work out where your home or school is on MAP **A**. Describe how close you are to an earthquake high-risk area.

What if...?

Wales rocked by an earthquake **B**

Britain's earthquakes cause little damage. Most of the tremors are too deep to shake the surface. But in case there is a big earthquake, the Government held a conference to see how Britain could cope. It was called 'Fantasy Catastrophe'. It had an imaginary earthquake at Elan, mid-Wales, August 1995. One year later the people of nearby Llandrindod Wells really did feel an earthquake!

> **LLANDRINDOD WELLS:** Doors and windows rattled yesterday in mid-Wales during an earthquake measuring 2.9 on the Richter Scale. The British Geological Survey in Edinburgh received about 20 reports from people woken by the quake at 5 a.m. The centre catalogues between 10 and 20 earthquakes of a similar size each year in the UK. The earthquake's epicentre was in a rural area about 7 km north east of Llandrindod Wells, Powys.
>
> *Leicester Mercury, 21 September 1996*

2 Read ARTICLE **B**.
  a Describe the location of the earthquake's epicentre.
  b How large was the earthquake?
  c How many other earthquakes of this size take place in the UK each year?
  d Suggest why the damage was small.

3 Study MAP **C**.
  a Compare the location of Elan to Llandrindod Wells.
  b What size was the 'Fantasy Catastrophe' earthquake?
  c Look back to the Richter Scale on page 76 to find out what damage it might cause.

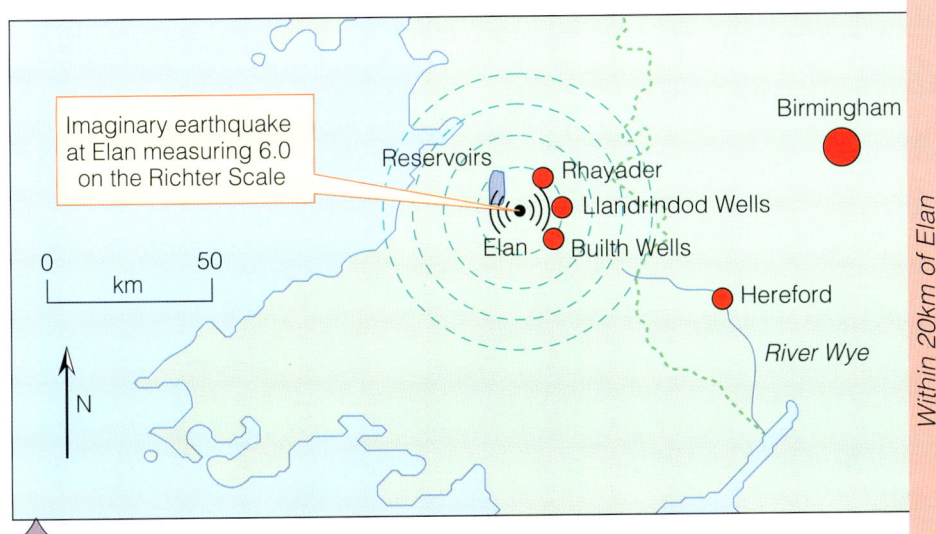

Imaginary earthquake at Elan measuring 6.0 on the Richter Scale

Reservoirs • Rhayader • Llandrindod Wells • Elan • Builth Wells • Birmingham • Hereford • River Wye

0 — 50 km

N

C Fantasy Catastrophe at Elan, Wales

Within 20km of Elan:
- People in Rhayader (pop. 2000), Llandrindod Wells (4300) and Builth Wells (1000) will all be affected.
- Buildings will collapse or be completely damaged.
- Falling materials will kill people.
- Roads and bridges will break.
- Gas, water, electricity, telephone and sewage pipes will be destroyed.
- Five reservoirs supplying water will be damaged. Waves may be 30 m high and travel at 20 m per second. After 2 hours, water will sweep over people, sheep and buildings as far as Builth Wells.

More than 20km:
- Further away, Hereford will be flooded by the River Wye.
- Birmingham's water supply from the reservoirs will be cut off.

The Times, 21 August 1995

D Scientists predict that...

4 Read the predictions in **D**.
  a Use a copy of a map that shows the location of your home or school. Draw a circle that represents a 20 km radius.
  b Describe the different land uses within this circle.
  c Imagine that an earthquake like Elan's happened close to your home or school. You and your family survive. Produce the front page of a newspaper reporting the disaster. Remember to refer to your local area within 20 km of your home or school.

Earthquakes & Volcanoes glossary

Adobe
Clay brick used for houses in hot countries.

Atmosphere
The layer of gases above the Earth where our weather takes place.

Convection current
Heat flow that moves **mantle** materials from a hot area to a cold area.

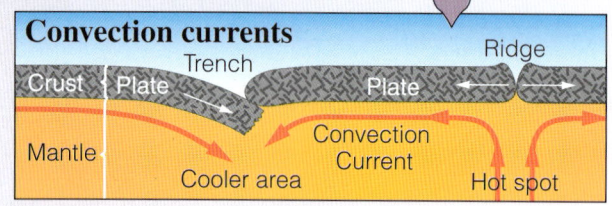

Convection currents
Trench — Ridge
Crust | Plate — Plate
Mantle — Cooler area — Convection Current — Hot spot

Core
The centre of the Earth.

Crust
The solid outside layer of the Earth which forms ocean floors and continents.

Epicentre
The place on the Earth's surface above the focus.

Erosion
The wearing away of the surface of the Earth by wind, rain, ice, rivers, and the sea.

Extrusive rocks
Rocks produced by the cooling of lava on the Earth's surface. Because they cooled quickly, they have small crystals e.g. basalt.

Basalt
1 cm

Focus
The place beneath the Earth's **crust** where an earthquake starts.

Igneous rocks
Rocks produced by the cooling of molten (melted) material.

Intrusive rocks
Rocks produced by the cooling of **magma** under the Earth's surface. Because they cooled slowly, they have large crystals e.g. granite.

Granite
1 cm

Lava
Molten (melted) rock on the Earth's surface.

Magma
Molten (melted) rock beneath the surface of the Earth.

Mantle
Semi-liquid hot material between the Earth's **crust** and its **core**.

Mid-Atlantic Ridge
A ridge under the Atlantic Ocean where two **plates** are moving apart.

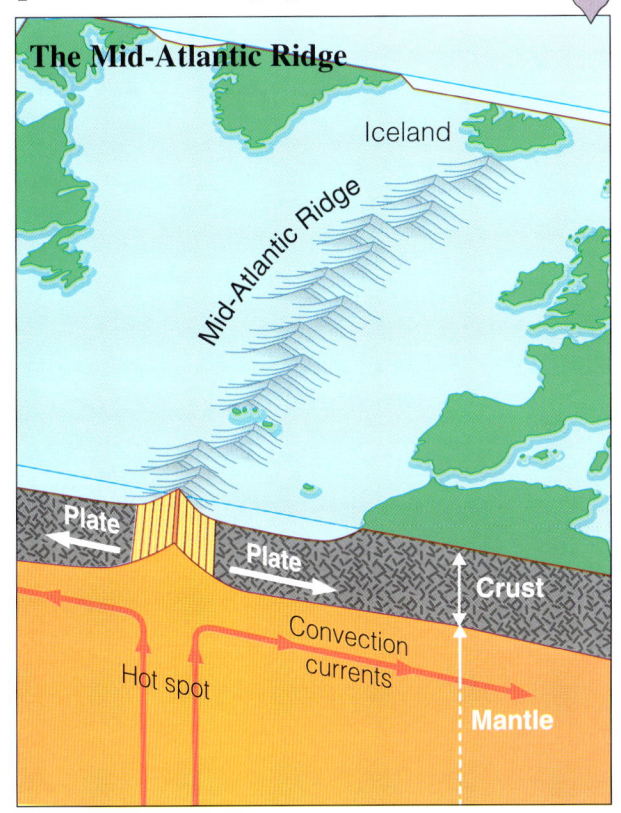

Plate
A solid **crust** that 'floats' on the **mantle**.

Plate boundary
Where two plates meet.

Ridge
The **plate boundary** where two plates are moving apart. New crust forms at a ridge.

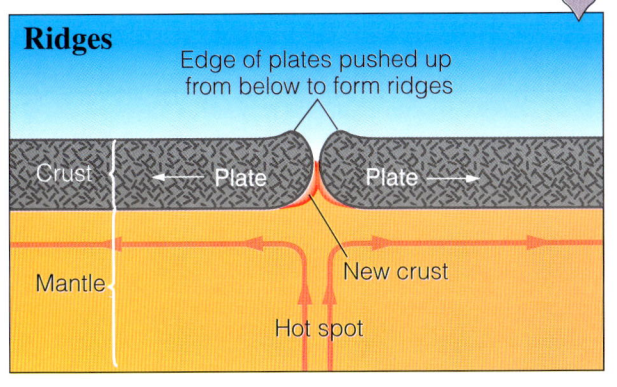

Satellite
Equipment launched into space to collect information about the Earth (or other planets).

Seismograph
A recording, usually on paper, of earthquake shock waves.

Seismologists
Scientists who study earthquakes.

Tremors
When the surface of the Earth shakes because of shock waves from earthquakes.

Trench
The **plate boundary** where one plate slides beneath the other. Crust is destroyed at a trench.

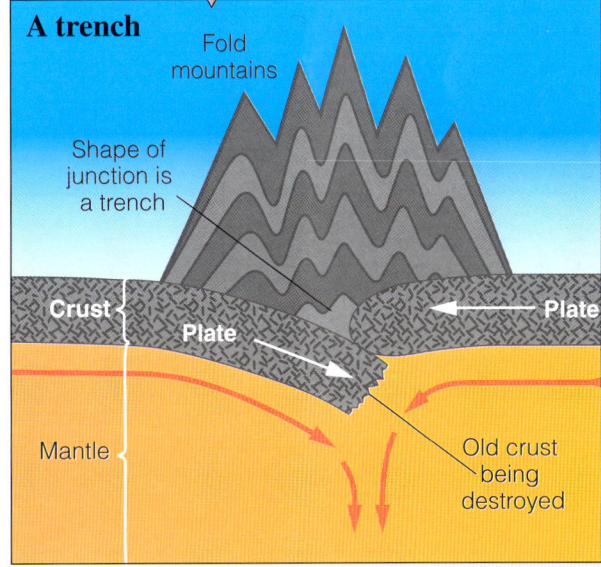

Weathering
The breaking up of rocks at the Earth's surface.

Vulcanologists
Scientists who study volcanoes.

The next step is yours ...

There are many different resources where you can find out about earthquakes and volcanoes.

A *After months of silence, Mt Ruapehu erupted today sending up plumes of ash and rock. Aviation authorities are forced to declare a danger zone across much of North Island, while ski resorts in the area have closed.*

New Zealand television news announcement, 17 June 1996

B *India accepted foreign aid yesterday as the death toll from the Maharashtra earthquake rose to 40 000. The quake measured 6.4 on the Richter Scale. Britain has already given £400 000 for medicine. The relief effort came as Indian experts – still puzzled by the quake – warned of another major one this winter.*

Newspaper report by Michael Atchinson, The Mail on Sunday, 3 October 1993

C Studying information on a computer

D Working in the library

---

1 Refer to RESOURCES **A–D**.
  a List where you could find out about earthquakes and volcanoes.
  b Suggest other ways in which you could get extra information.

2 Look back through this unit.
  a Choose an earthquake or a volcanic eruption that interests you. You could find a different example from another source if you prefer.
  b Prepare a wall display on your choice. Your display should answer these four questions:
  • Where did it take place? (Draw a map.)
  • Why did it happen? (Draw diagrams if they help.)
  • What damage did it do?
  • How did people and organisations respond?

3 Prepare a two-minute talk to present to your teacher and classmates. It should explain why you produced the display in the way you did.

What's next?

Rivers and coasts

France

GEOGRAPHY Direct

2 Gary Cambers
Stuart Currie

Work and employment

Ecosystems

Published by Collins Educational
An imprint of HarperCollins *Publishers*
77-85 Fulham Palace Road
London W6 8JB

© HarperCollins Publishers 1998

First published 1998

Reprinted 2000

ISBN 0 00 3266974

Gary Cambers and Stuart Currie assert the moral right to be identified as the authors of this work.

All rights reserved. No part of this publication may be reproduced, stored in a retrieval system, or transmitted in any form or by any means, electronic, mechanical, photocopying, recording or otherwise, without either the prior permission of the Publisher or a licence permitting restricted copying in the United Kingdom issued by the Copyright Licensing Agency Ltd, 90 Tottenham Court Road, London W1P 9HE.

British Library Cataloguing in Publication Data

A catalogue record for this book is available from the British Library.

Edited by Anne Montefiore

Design, cover design and artwork by Ken Vail Graphic Design

Illustrations by Judy Brown, Simon Girling & Associates (Mike Lacey)

Picture research by Lucy Courtenay and Tamsin Miller

Production by Sue Cashin

Printed and bound by
Printing Express Ltd., Hong Kong.

The authors and Publisher are especially grateful to Carol Cambers for her contributions in the writing of this book. They would like to thank her for her support.

This book contains references to characters in case studies. For educational purposes only, photographs have been used to accompany these case studies. The juxtaposition of photographs and case studies is not intended to identify the individual in the photograph with the character in the case study. The publishers cannot accept any responsibility for any consequences resulting from this use of photographs and case studies, except as expressly provided by law.

Acknowledgements

Every effort has been made to contact the holders of copyright material, but if any have been overlooked, the publishers will be pleased to make the necessary arrangements at the first opportunity.

PHOTOGRAPHS

The publishers would like to thank the following for permission to reproduce photographs:

Cover photograph by Tony Stone Images/Paul Harris: Hikers resting on Scafell, Cumbria, England

Items are listed under unit headings by spread number and resource letter, unless otherwise stated with page number and/or additional listings as (T) = Top, (B) = Bottom, (C) = Centre, (L) = Left, (R) = Right.

Page 4 Telegraph Colour Library

Settlement

Stuart Currie page 5(T), page 5(C), 2C, 2D, 4A, 4B, 4C, 4E, 5C, 5D, 6B, 6C, 6D, 6E, 6F, 6G, 7B, 8E (L), 8E (R), 10A, 10C, 10D, 10E, 10F, 11A, 11B, 11C, 11D, 11E, 11F, 12B, 12E, 12H, 13D, 13F, 14B, 14D (L), 14D (R), 14E, 14F, glossary (TC), glossary (BC), glossary (B), page 36(L), page 36(R); Duncan Stacey 1B, 1C, 1D; Sally and Richard Greenhill 1E; Ely Cathedral 2E; Bluecoat Press Liverpool 2F; London Aerial Photo Library 2G; G. Wallis 3B(L); Bridgeman Art Library 3B(B); Hulton Deutsch Collection 3B(T); Raleigh Industries 3B(C); Nottingham Evening Post 3B(L); John Birdsall 7A, 7D(L), 7D(R); The Vintage Magazine Co. Archive 9A, 9B; D. Currie 8F, 10B; Collections/Alain le Garsmeur glossary (T); Asaad Raoof, Nottingham City Council, Design & Property Services 13E; Adtranz 13G;

Population

Stuart Currie page 39(R), 3C, 3F, 4B (C), 4B (R), 4C, 4D, 11A, 11B 11C, 11D, Tony Stone Images page 39(L), 1C, 10C; Still Pictures 1E (Mark Edwards), 2C (Paul Harrison), 2D (Mark Edwards); Biofotos (Heather Angel) 1B, (Brian Rogers) 1D; Panos Pictures (Neil Cooper) 2E; Prodeepta Das 3D, 4B (L), 4E; Vintage Magazine Company 6E; John Birdsall 6D; Horst W. Böhne 6F; Keith Smalley 7B; EuroVillages 7F; Bridgeman Art Library 8A(L), 8A(C); Dept of Photography, Printing & Design, UMDS, Guyís Hospital 8A(T); Telegraph Colour Library 8A(R), 9B, page 64; J Allan Cash 9C; Carlisle Marketing Board 9E; Gareth Price 12A; Lucy Courtenay 12B; Greg Evans International Photo Library 12C; Images Colour Library 12D; Mark Edwards/Still pictures glossary (L); Tim Booth glossary (R)

Earthquakes & Volcanoes

Kyodo News page 65(L); Scott Lee, Whakapapa Ski Area page 65(R); Popperfoto 1C, 1D, 5B, 7B, 7C, 7E(L), 7E(R), 10E, page 94A, page 94B; Oxford Scientific Films 1B, 10B; Hulton Deutsch Collection 2D; Science Photo Library 3C, 6D, 12A (C), glossary (R); Portuguese Trade and Tourism Office 4B; Tim Booth 7A; Associated Press 8D; Hashimoto-Sygma 8C (L); Japan Information and Cultural Centre 8C (R); Times Newspapers Ltd 9A; Landcare Research New Zealand Ltd. 11A; Tony Stone Images 11E, page 95(TL); Collections 12A (Michael Diggin TL, Ed Gabriel TR, Brian Shuel BL, Geogre Wright BR); GeoScience Features Picture Library glossary (L), glossary (C); Telegraph Colour Library page 94 C, D; Page 95 Christine Osborne Pictures (BR), (BL); Telegraph Colour Library (TR); Tony Stone (TL); 12E reproduced by kind permission of The European. 'Das Ruhrgebiet' logo on page 48 reproduced by kind permission of the Kommunalverband Ruhrgebiet, Essen.

MAPS

11G reproduced from Landranger Map 129, Nottingham and Loughborough area 1996 Ordnance Survey 1:50000 map with the permission of the Controller of Her Majesty's Stationery Office, © Crown Copyright.